FOLKTALES
from the Helotes Settlement

FOLKTALES
from the Helotes Settlement

JOHN IGO

Edited by
Kenneth L. Untiedt

Illustrated by Scott Runnels

Texas Folklore Society Extra Book Number 25

UNT PRESS

University of North Texas Press
Denton, Texas

Printed in the United States of America.

10 9 8 7 6 5 4 3 2 1

Permissions:
University of North Texas Press
1155 Union Circle #311336
Denton, TX 76203-5017

The paper used in this book meets the minimum requirements of the American National Standard for Permanence of Paper for Printed Library Materials, z39.48.1984. Binding materials have been chosen for durability.

Library of Congress Cataloging-in-Publication Data

Igo, John, 1927- author.
Folktales from the Helotes settlement / John Igo ; edited by Kenneth L. Untiedt ; illustrated by Scott Runnels. — Edition: First.
pages cm — (Texas Folklore Society extra book ; number 25)
ISBN 978-1-57441-589-6 (cloth : alk. paper) — ISBN 978-1-57441-590-2 (ebook)
1. Helotes (Tex.)—Folklore. 2. Helotes (Tex.)—History—20th century—Anecdotes. 3. Helotes (Tex.)—Social life and customs—20th century—Anecdotes. I. Untiedt, Kenneth L., 1966- editor. II. Title. III. Series: Texas Folklore Society extra book ; no. 25.
GR110.T5I46 2014
976.4'35—dc23
2014033771

Folktales from the Helotes Settlement is Texas Folklore Society Extra Book Number 25

The electronic edition of this book was made possible by the support of the Vick Family Foundation.

CONTENTS

PREFACE

John Igo first approached me with the idea for this book when I was putting together *Celebrating 100 Years* (PTFS #66), but at that time I was only able to use one of the pieces, "The 4th of July." Nothing more came of it until he called me one day in the fall of 2013, asking if I was still interested in doing something with the entire manuscript. Admittedly, I had not been, if only because it was a short manuscript, much shorter than anything we had done before as a complete book. However, it just so happened that Ron Chrisman, the Director of the UNT Press, had talked to me about another manuscript very similar to John's not long before that, and the idea of packaging a couple of books together turned into the idea of packaging a *few* books together.

Thus, *Folktales from the Helotes Settlement* became the twenty-fifth Extra Book for the Texas Folklore Society. Members received it as part of their dues for 2014, along with Joyce Gibson Roach's *Short Call: Snippets from the Little Bittiest Places in Texas* and *Dog Trots and Mud Houses. Dog Trots* was originally published in 1979, and Ron generously agreed to give leftover copies to TFS members as a bonus publication.

Why publish these anecdotes? Well, these stories capture the lore of a place similar to many, many other places—*our* places. Here we find legends, mysteries, beliefs of the people of the Helotes Settlement. They're familiar to us all, because we have our own ghost stories, legendary figures, unique characters, and town lore. We remember; we share; we continue the traditions and the customs. In short, we can relate.

As I did with Joyce's book, I want to thank several people for their part in bringing this book to print. First, I thank not only Ron Chrisman, but also Karen DeVinney and the rest of the staff members at the UNT Press who help us put these books together each year. I want to show special gratitude to a couple of people at Stephen F. Austin State University who continue to generously support the Society, including Mark Sanders, the Chair of the English Department, and Brian Murphy, the Dean of the College of Liberal and Applied Arts. In addition to these individuals, I thank all the other administrators and my colleagues who make us glad to call SFA and Nacogdoches home. I'm especially grateful for Scott Runnels, a friend and an instructor in the School of Art at SFA, who signed on and provided the illustrations for the book.

I again thank Mary Margaret Gonzales, who stayed with me and kept me focused as this project grew. She has definitely done her fair share to put this volume together; it has been a complex job at times, but working together has made the process much easier.

This is John's book, and he has dedicated it to those who served as inspiration to him. If anything, I add my thanks to him and his continued love for and service to the Texas Folklore Society—for more years than any other member. Kudos, John.

Kenneth L. Untiedt
Stephen F. Austin State University
Nacogdoches, Texas
May 16, 2014

INTRODUCTION AND DEDICATION

The family had lived on the land since the 1870s, but we lived in a depression-era, cobbled-together, shiplap frame house at the end of a private dirt road fourteen miles northwest of San Antonio.

Until we got electricity from the R. E. A. in Boerne we had a coal-oil cook stove and lamps. A Delco battery-powered radio owned by a nearby relative was useless—there were no news programs then. We heard big news only when someone else went somewhere.

But we had something outsiders generally did not have—our supper table and its visitors. It was an unspoken and unbroken rule that all family members came to the table for supper, even when they weren't going to eat. We had adult talk: stories, history, grapevine, family lore. Our only entertainment was tale-telling. Truth or Facts were not a concern.

Fate helped. My mother, the youngest daughter of ten children, had gradually become the family historian and the *tribe* told her its tale and then, to be safe, her siblings. Our extended family, friends, and neighbors told her things in detail with names, dates, specific locations. And she had a retentive mind. Even years later, on request (at the table or elsewhere) she could retell the whole thing.

Also, we had her brother, George Woller, a fabulist tale-teller, who could turn any situation into a story. Later, he had a high fever which, despite ice packs and wet sheets, "cooked his brain" and left him obviously dimmed, yet made his recollections more vivid but untrustworthy except for details (particulars).

And our great-uncle, Joe Gerfers, was a humorous storyteller, who told tales usually about victims, including himself.

At the table we heard new stories and old ones repolished. We were grateful to have visitors. We entertained them with our cornucopia of oral hand-me-downs.

There was no pecking order. And nobody complained that others corrected details; ("That egg was plaster-of-paris, not glass; someone always added, "Damn snake, poor snake.") Everyone accepted that the story had to be kept right.

The kid spoke up only to ask questions or ask for more, and more.

One summer, a couple of decades later, while I was telling my oldest niece some of our best stories, the thought came that *someone* should write them down. Several years after that I had a second thought: I am someone; it is my job to write them down or they will be lost.

The table and its clan are long gone now. The house is still there, but it is in San Antonio and, worse, it is cut off from the Settlement by Loop 1604.

Only these tales remain with nobody left to correct them. That atypically silent kid was like his mother, a cultural sponge.

These are the squeezings.

John Igo
San Antonio, Texas
February 24, 2014

THE WHITE CHAPEL

Drivers outbound on Bandera Road toward San Geronimo noticed activity up top of a hill to their right, two hills past the Catholic Cemetery. It slowly became a white chapel, apparently only about the size of four telephone booths.

Since it had never been mentioned, of course they stopped and asked the nearest homeowner. His response became legendary. He said, "My wife and I prayed when our son left for Korea: 'Please God, if you let him come home, we will build a little white chapel for your mother.' He died in Korea, and they shipped him home to Fort Sam. So we are building the chapel for His mother, where people can see it from far off. We got our son. We just weren't smart enough to say, 'Alive.'"

HITZFELDER

It didn't take decades or even years. Arthur Hitzfelder was the Game Warden, and he became a living myth almost immediately.

Stories about him were everywhere. Some hunters apparently believed he could be several places at the same time. He'd arrest a poacher in the Culebra, another in Somerset, and another in Selma—all in the same day. They all *knew* that.

He made scofflaws uneasy, almost panicky. Some posted lookouts with flashlight signals. One knew he had arrested a headlighter over close to the county line, off Bandera Road, so he believed he was safe the next evening. Wrong.

Hitzfelder sort of specialized in deer. He did fish, also. He arrested one man for having a five-cell D-size flashlight in his truck—what could it be used for if not for headlighting? The man confessed, and his flashlight was confiscated. He stopped a car with a buck on the roof, to check the tag, and found a spike buck in the trunk. Another man had three bucks and tags only for two.

He wasn't disliked. He was feared.

One hunter over Leon Springs way offered him a bribe, "just between us." That got him handcuffs, a fine, and jail time.

Hunters believed that he couldn't be outwitted. That was a challenge in itself. They tried. One man had been careful. While he was gutting an out-of-season buck in a field screened by trees, he heard footsteps and saw a downward-pointing flashlight. Hitzfelder.

Hitzfelder was Game Warden for years, but his legends, usually not specific, made his time seem much longer. The "steely-eyed" lawman not only enforced the law, but by his larger-than-life folk image prevented law-breaking. Hunters said that he would arrest his own grandmother. What he could not prevent or control was the kaleidoscope of memories, lies, guesses, and downright superstitions attached to his name.

His name was Hitzfelder, but for blame (late) or praise (late) everyone called him just Hitzfelder. Arthur was never used, and maybe hunters didn't know it.

Nobody knew if he had a wife somewhere—he was all over the country at all hours. (Some believed that he never slept.) A wife at home didn't seem likely; the only fact that they could get was that his uncle owned and ran a saloon at San Marcos and Morales streets on the near-west side in San Antonio.

In Jim's, over hot apple pie and coffee, an amused man remembered a family story:

"My grandfather hated him. Hitzfelder arrested Granddad three times in three years in the same box-canyon, when he meant for Hitzfelder to be over toward Selma. To make sure, Granddad called in to report headlighting over by Coker Methodist. That Hitzfelder was too sharp for him. Hitzfelder told Granddad that his tip was too easy—obviously somebody wanted him out of the way. It was an easy guess, since the lead placed the law-breaking in the Coker Cemetery. So he came north of Helotes instead. Made Granddad feel like a fool. At home he called Hitzfelder a damn busybody."

Hitzfelder died, aged 89, in 1991 after a long retirement. Young hunters did not know him. Old-timers remembered him vividly and told stories about him.

And because Hitzfelder did not die on the job, old-time hunters felt somehow cheated.

WHAT TOLL ROAD?

[Note: There is almost no folklore about this subject. It was "invisible" mostly, except to outsiders.]

Joe and Lorraine Van De Walle of the Van De Walle Farms, co-owned a house on top of a hill above Medina Lake, facing the nearby Medina Dam. They went back and forth a lot, and saved about an hour each way, each time. They went from Culebra Road (FM 471) to the toll road.

What toll road?

The enterprising Schuhards owned a great swath of land between Helotes and Medina Lake. They made the toll road, a hard dirt but mostly gravel road that sliced through flatlands and woods, over cattle guards at fence lines and through one bumpgate.

They put up a flagstone toll house at the Helotes end. In 2011, it was still standing. Pat Driscoll was planning an article on it for the *San Antonio Express-News,* but that didn't happen. At the Lake end there was another toll booth, now gone or drastically renovated.

Helping a researcher, Irene McCrystal stopped to ask a "local" about the booth and the road. He was a Schuhard who gave her information about the Lake-end tolling. Tolling worked both ways, of course.

The tolls made very little money, not enough to maintain a road. The road was a generous public service. Traffic improved. The few versions of tales about it (from Lorraine Van De Walle and others) disagree: 25¢ per person, 25¢ per car, other amounts—but all coins.

Helotes locals, many "hard-headed" second generation Germans, would not pay a toll. They chose to go out Bandera to Hwy. 377, or even to Pipe Creek and then turn to get to the Lake. And save money.

The Helotes-end toll house sits back, now, from the widened road, backed into a house. Drivers, finding nobody in the toll house, honked, and a lady (some say named Hazel) came from the house. It was, basically, an honor system.

Then (Driscoll had all the details) the county (or state?) government bought the right-of-way, improved it, and gave it a number: 1383. And Medina Lake became easily accessible. There was no more tolling. With 1383 in operation the toll road became invisible.

The Schuhard toll road must have started early, soon after the Dam was constructed. It was in full operation in the 1930s.

At that time, Texas had only two toll roads, both privately owned. One was from Laredo to Eagle Pass or Del Rio. It starved to death. People took state and county roads instead. The owners tried to sell stock; they tried to sell the road to corporations as an investment. It died and disappeared. Local governments were uninterested.

The other was the Schuhard toll road, known as the Medina Lake Toll Road. It faded into the landscape.

Now people, including Helotes area residents, ask: "What toll road?"

FREDDIE AT MAUD'S

Maud Fuller ran a long, narrow grocery store. Up front she had the icebox-refrigerator and a few tables with odd chairs, a café—*the* café. Sandwiches, drinks, and a daily plate lunch of her choosing. If someone wanted a sandwich, he said cheese, ham, or baloney. She carved the choice off big rolls, slapped the choice between two slices of store-bought bread with no trimmings. That was it. Functional only.

Freddie Biering, who owned property on both sides of what is now the Bandera Road-Loop 1604 intersection, was a deadpan kidder. Once for an all-you-can-eat special, he ordered a special and a dozen oranges. Maud had asked, "Want anything else?" He told her no, that the oranges were for dessert.

Another day, Freddie said, he went to Maud's and ordered "Just coffee." She poured, and poured again. He pointed at his cup. She poured again. After six cups, she made the mistake of asking about. "Freddie, you sure must like my coffee."

"Not particularly. It's just that you have to drink so much to get any."

SHAVANO

The richest name for folktales near Helotes is Shavano (SHAV-a-no). Nobody knows, but everybody has an opinion. "I suppose . . ." is the frequent opening of another fantasized source.

At the eastern edge of the Settlement, near where it would overlap the Shavano Settlement area, was a "filling station" that served as a primitive convenience store. It offered red or white gasoline pumped up into a glass cylinder marked with painted gallon marks. It offered coal-oil (four turns of the handle dispensed a gallon into your container). Inside, canned chili beans was a favorite. It offered other food essentials. And for a few years it served as a lunch-only café with a minimal menu. It also offered bottles of Virginia Dare (sweet) wine any day at any time, except Sunday mornings. On Sunday mornings buyers (regulars only) would hear, "You left this package yesterday." It was a brown bag.

It also had—shh!—a slot machine that would disappear from the counter when any stranger came in. It was a diversion for workers homebound after their shift at Camp Stanley. It also had two kinds of punch boards, one with a metal puncher to get a folded number; the other was a peel-off-the-name board with ladies' names. All three paid off, but never much.

That business was named Shavano. It stood at the corner where Hausman Road dead-ends in Fredericksburg Road, where a car dealership now is. If anyone in the Settlement said, "I'm going (out) to Shavano," that was the destination.

The earliest proprietors, in folk history, were Jack Battersby and his wife, Violet Bacon. They were followed by their daughter, Bennie Bee, and her husband, Weir. Then there's a blur. Some think they remember another couple, an Anglo with a reclusive Hispanic wife. Then the Blakes took over.

The Blakes added the café and hired Mrs. Blake's sister, Mrs. Magee, as their cook and waitress for their five- or six-table operation. Mr. Blake added the under-the-table gambling devices. He also served as a postal drop-off station for area packages that wouldn't fit in regulation mail boxes.

That was the concrete, real Shavano, which died when Mr. Blake died, and his son, Jim, moved the business to Huebner at Babcock and named it Jim's Corner.

To the east of Fredericksburg Road, south of Blake's corner, lies an area now known as Shavano Park. There is also a Shavano Road, and a subdivision bears the name.

Up the hill at the De Zavala House was the Shavano Post Office (run by A. De Zavala). Ruby Boldt Maytum has an envelope bearing the postmark "Shavano, Texas." There was also a flag-stop railroad station just south of De Zavala Road, close to the southern end of the Clark High School campus.

But folklore can't be stifled. The origin of the name tantalizes, and provokes colorful guessing. Indians, of course: it is always Indians first.

But those Indians can't be found in any historical record people hear: They died out. They were killed off (ah, those gun-slits in the De Zavala basement!). There were no intermarriages and nobody to claim Shavano heritage. There have been no Shavano living or burial sites. Without a trace.

The most reasonable explanation is colorful and also untrustworthy. Out of San Antonio *way* back (to the Republic?) there was a (choose one: Captain, Major, General) Cheveneaux, somehow connected to Francisco Guilbeau who was the French Consul (or the like). Cheveneaux bought or was given acreage in what is now the Shavano area.

He had Indians from San Antonio working for him. They were known as Cheveneaux Indians. Bingo! They became, after the fact, Shavano Indians. (They weren't, but the name caught on.) Old-timers in the Helotes Settlement had not heard of the Indians. They were never mentioned.

But the name was known all over.

THE MOBILE MARKET

In the early days the Settlement had merchants gathering monthly with their wagons full of wares. Progress made a major change.

One of the Brauchle sons, a brother of Henry the sheep man, created a mobile meat market. In the bed of a primitive pickup truck, about 1930, he installed the equivalent of a camper shell, lined with cork, with sealed-off crevices. He added a metal trough to hold a big block of ice (with an outside drain). He opened shop. He drove to his customers on a regular schedule.

It was practical for him to visit Stringtown weekly, starting at the north (Benke) end. Just in Stringtown he could sell out.

He offered several kinds of fresh steaks, roasts, and chopped beef—no hamburger. He offered pork roasts, pork loins, and pork chops. He also had goat meat or mutton, usually hind legs. He didn't sell sausage, either.

He did not carve or trim anything on sale. It was all pre-cut to be wrapped in butcher paper.

But he also sold (shh!) "dark meat," a code name for venison. Selling venison was/is illegal at all times. But it was available in quantity, especially during deer season (ah, venison chili!).

If there was a car or truck at a regular customer's house, he would bypass it till later. The fear of Hitzfelder was strong.

He served throughout the Settlement. Sadly, sometime by the late 1930s he went out of business. At least, he didn't come back to Stringtown.

STATIONS OF THE CROSS

A few miles up the road from central Helotes was the Catholic Church known as Los Reyes, a simple wooden structure where the circuit-riding Catholic priest said Mass regularly—although not necessarily weekly. He performed weddings, baptized infants, heard confessions before Mass, visited the bedridden, and acted as pastor.

But for reasons never explained, the Catholic bishop sold the building to a Protestant church in San Antonio. Feelings ran deep.

The building was jacked up and some sort of rollers were installed. It was ready for trailers and oxen or mules to pull it.

Then the night before it was to be towed, mysteriously it burned to the ground. Parishioners were openly grateful. But nobody ever found out who did it—even though "everyone" knew it was arson and not, as some wished, an act of God.

Skip forward about fifteen years.

The new church, Our Lady of Guadalupe, was built on land donated by Catherine Antonio, along Bandera, on the portion now renamed Riggs Road. The first pastor,

Alfred Rabe, S.M., came weekly for Sunday Masses, from St. Mary's University, where earlier he had been President. One week soon after the church was consecrated by a new bishop, Father Rabe opened the front door and found all the Stations of the Cross stacked and leaning against the Gospel side of the altar.

At Mass old-timers recognized the Stations from Los Reyes. Everybody was comfortable with that, an auspicious sign for the young parish, even though it confirmed the belief that it had been arson.

Skip ahead about another ten years.

Father Cyril Kuehne, S.M., was pastor. We had a large (30" by 50") framed fine print of Our Lady of Guadalupe in the parish hall, which was going to be remodeled. Rather than make plans for it, Father Kuehne decided to give it away. He asked for suggestions from the Altar Society, the Holy Name Society, and parishioners at large.

I reminded him that the Johnny Rosas family had been doing our janitorial work for years as their weekly offering—father, mother, two daughters, and a son. Instead of money, they offered their services, sweeping, mopping as necessary, dusting the pews, replacing candles as necessary, and washing windows.

Instantly he agreed, and the next Sunday, after the 9:30 Mass, in the parish hall, father presented the nicely-framed Guadalupe to the Rosas family. There was warm support. There were no negative murmurs. Father, it turned out, had not asked anyone else. The first suggestion was "right."

Sometime after that, Leo Schott asked how I came to suggest Johnny Rosas. Father had told him before a Holy Name meeting.

"Their major service. And anyhow, I think that it was Johnny who saved the Stations."

Leo twinkled. Yes, Johnny deserved it. Good choice. "But," he added, "suppose it was a group, three close friends who would never tell on the others? Arson is a felony." He walked back to talk with his lifelong good friends, Red Haby and brother, Howard.

Four of them, then?

JOHN MARNOCK'S DOG

John Marnock, brother of "D. Marnock" on Scenic Loop Road, had a cottage (since renovated and still standing many decades later) on Bandera Road halfway to Leon Valley and the Onion House.

John and his dog, a Border Collie, walked up Bandera Road through Helotes, to visit Gabriel Marnock. Then they would walk back home.

One day John felt sick. He wrote a note, wrapped it in oil paper and tied it securely to a short stick. He gave it to the dog and (evidently) told him to take it to Gabriel. The dog left with the stick in his mouth, up Bandera Road, through Helotes, onto the Scenic Loop Road and to the Marnock House. There he made enough noise to bring someone to the front door. Gabriel was home. Immediately he had his children back his fast pony into the shafts of his light two-wheeler. The dog jumped up beside him and they left.

John was dead when they arrived. He had left a note, giving the dog to Gabriel.

Every now and then the dog would disappear for a day. Nobody knew where. Maybe back home? No. Then someone reported seeing him in the cemetery, lying by a grave, they said.

THE OTHER BARBER

He was too young to be a legend—and he was an outsider. But Pete managed.

Pete, Pedro Adame, was restless, energetic, optimistic. When he left the military, he went to barber college. He was not going to take orders ever again. He would be his own boss. He opened a shop on Bandera Road, well inside Loop 410. His prices undercut other shops' prices. He had a phone call from "Uncle" Ed Lagleder, who was a power in the barbers' union. Pete wouldn't join; he'd have to accept their guidelines.

He had another phone call mentioning (oh, so offhandedly) that "we" knew where his children were going to school. That made Pete stubborn. The answer was still No. Nobody could tell Pete what to do. A voice on the phone told him that if he raised his prices to match the union's prices, he wouldn't have to join. NO. Pete would set his own prices.

Then one night someone smashed his shop window, poured a flammable liquid in, and set the shop on fire. Coincidence.

He moved into an available space in the Strange Center on Bandera Road at Hillcrest Drive.

Outraged friends, neighbors, and regulars offered to "sit shotgun" on the shop. Pete said No.

Then he found a space in Helotes, adjoining the Rock Store, a space that had been the U.S. Post Office and a temporary bookstore when the Poore family sold used or discarded library books.

His powerful competition, owned and operated by Ella Sanchez Dunford, a Woller cousin whose Helotes roots ran deep—she was the daughter of legendary Celestino Sanchez. That was formidable as a challenge. Pete never wavered.

His customers were newcomers, some who knew about the fire, and some men who didn't like waiting in a shop where there were women barbers. And Ella's had a beauty shop through an archway from the barbershop. A male thing.

Pete's barbershop had no mirrors.

Pete was restless. He added a shop in the unused half of his rented space, with two long pipe racks of cleaned and pressed clothes (by Mrs. Pete?) and shoes. His customers included (shhh!) "wetbacks."

Dora Benke Naegelin had two summer seasonal wetbacks working for her, building or repairing fences. She and Annie Igo took the two to Pete's, where the men bought clothes. But, even with Pete's prices, they were short of cash and asked if they could come back for shoes next payday. Dora and Annie bought them two pairs of shoes each. Pete donated one denim jacket each.

Then Pete added useful items for the home or workplace: jumper cables, tool kits, hammers, pliers, spikes, all items he had picked up, new, on Sundays at the Moursund Road Flea Market in southern San Antonio.

About that time Pete began to gain weight. People supposed it was success and beer. Pete was thin-framed, but his middle soon outgrew his guayaberas. He picked up some "irregular" but new white lab jackets at Moursunds, large size.

Then Pete took on another line. He had read that there was a flourishing market in coins for collectors and investors. Pete bought two glass-topped cases and offered American coins only. He could talk about the various mints and the like. He sold most of them and restocked.

He was physically restless, too. He'd turn the chair for no apparent reason and then move to match it, several times during each haircut.

A customer suggested that Pete go see a (free) VA doctor about his enlarged belly. NO. He'd decide whether he'd go, and when.

Then the new Pete evolved. He became a lecturer, a monologist on his topic of the day. He'd stop and gesture with a comb, a sweep, and a jab. He talked about politics, economics, health laws, social issues, funds for schools. No sports, no hunting, no local gossip. He'd pause, instrument in hand, to get his ideas straight, and then start up again. Customers didn't complain. Pete, ever fatter, became the Village Philosopher.

Then, without warning, Pete didn't open his shop one Tuesday. A week passed.

Then the word came. After a week or two or three, Pete had died of stomach and other cancers. Only his landlord (the news bringer) and/or his family knew what had become of Pete's multivarious stock.

But men, even sitting in Ella's, still mention Pete's with affection.

THE DOWSER

Wilhelmina Zuelecke Woller, widow of Steve, lived near one end of Stringtown (explained later herein) on Babcock Road, across the road from her sister, Mrs. Hoffman. Fluent in English, they were even more fluent in German, speaking only German to each other.

Wilhelmina, "Mina," was small but feared. She lived in an ochre-colored wooden house (where University Baptist Church now is). She had a de-horned tan cow named Muley, a slow-spoken bachelor son, daughters (one who ran off to Schulenbeg to become a nun), a boardgame called Muhl, that is pronounced "Mill," and her dowsing rod.

That rod was the source of the fear. It was a forked stick without bark, about the size of a yoke used to prevent cows from going through fences (two or three feet long). It was aged wood, hard, light tan. It was the familiar peach dowsing rod.

She kept it, wrapped in heavy oilpaper and tied with twine—no metal, no rubber, on the rafters of her lean-to back porch. Nobody else ever touched it, not even her son, Charley.

Area farmers, ranchers, and homebuilders consulted her about where to drill for water. Legends claimed that she never missed. That's why she was feared. She walked the area, holding the two prongs. "Here." It was final. Ranchers had to reconfigure their cow lots to accommodate. They would have preferred "over there."

She also water-witched for dug wells. She talked of hardground and softground, under. She found the place. It was their problem, drilling or digging.

Stories sprung up. She was in a trance while she dowsed. She would not discuss where she got the rod.

If someone had tried dowsing with a coat hanger (straightened out and bent to form a U) she charged more.

Her mind impressed people, too. She was a stickler for logic, for the letter of the law. She advised newlyweds, "Get it in writing, black on white." People brought her contracts to read and explain, before they signed anything they thought important.

In her large chifferobe she kept her "old" dresses, ones she had worn back before the turn of the century. They were black, wasp-waisted, floor length, of course. They smelled of vetiver. And she lent two of them, once, to her niece, Annie Woller Igo, and to Alice Igo Bowman.

They wore them to a costume dance and tied for first place. They thanked her publicly.

She had, strangely, a soft spot for the little boy across the road in her rent house. She volunteered to babysit. She and Mrs. Hoffman taught him German. He never heard English from them, except with his parents present. She and Charley played Mill with him, using red beans and white beans.

She took a relative (which? but not family) for a walk. They went through the cow lot, past Muley, and turned into the woods to the north. She stopped at a tree, explained about hardground and softground. Then she warned the relative to memorize the landmarks (this tree, that tree, that rock, and that tree) so as to be able to find her tree again.

Why? Because under that ordinary surface, there was some money she had buried, that even Steve and Charley didn't know about.

She had another reputation. She made the best sauerkraut of Stringtown, in a heavy crock with a wooden loose lid that rattled while the cabbage was fermenting. Neighbors considered themselves lucky to get a Mason jar filled with sauerkraut. She also had a system for preserving pork chops in lard that nobody copied. Pork is dangerous. Hers wasn't.

She told the little boy about water. "There's water, under. It's alive and waiting. Dummkopfs should not mess with it. Don't douse—it does something to you." That scared him.

Years passed. She died.

The estate sale sold the Mill card from Germany. But her dowsing rod was missing. Maybe Charley took it? It was gone. And time had changed all the landmarks in the woods.

SPRING

[Note: This account comes in two versions, essentially the same, but with different names, Leo and Howard. This is the version Howard told on himself one Sunday at the Helotes Café, after the 9:30 Mass.]

There was a little spring that had been there since the Europeans came. It was not big, but it flowed. It supplied drinking water before a well was drilled.

Howard considered it. It would be better larger.

He widened the stream bed to handle the bigger flow. Then he had to consider a pool, tiny, one for goldfish, or a wide shallow reflecting pool. A wading pool, or even if he was lucky, a small swimming pool.

Then, being practical, he considered a dam, earthworks or concrete. That required a planned spillway to get the overflow back to its natural bed.

He talked about it, and friends and neighbors wondered whether it would be like the pool at Celestino Sanchez's (that pool even had a name, now lost). Would it have any special features, like the concrete steps in the Scenic Loop Playground?

He waited for "the right time."

One day it was the right time.

He went to the spring coming out between a shelf of rocks, with a stick of dynamite.

The flow stopped. He waited for the ground shock to wear off. No flow. With a tool (a crowbar?) he poked around in the hole, trying to dislodge whatever was blocking it. No flow.

Maybe the next day, he had to report to relatives, friends, and neighbors that he had to wait for the water table to come back up.

Days. No flow.

Everybody except Howard found it funny. He had ruined a good spring. He was teased: "I have a leaky water pipe under my water tank. Would you come fix it?" "The San Geronimo Creek sure could use a dam." "Is it illegal to destroy a natural water supply?" It went on and on. He took it pretty well. He even got to the point where he could tell the story to a group in a café. He laughed along with them.

And, to put the cherry on the sundae, he asked the waitress for a glass of water.

The laughter exploded, but not as bad as that stick of dynamite.

BY ANY OTHER NAME

Child mortality was high. Women did all they could without either doctors or medical supplies at hand. Even with midwives, births were precarious for mother and child.

So when Helena (Lena) gave birth to full-term but badly underweight twins, nobody would have been surprised if one or both died. She said later that they weighed "about three pounds each." Since they were full-term, the complications of premature birth weren't there.

She didn't have any rubbing alcohol. She made do with 90-proof liquor and bleach.

She bathed the babies with a cloth dipped in "likker." Surfaces were scrubbed with bleach. Their father was not allowed to pick them up. She boiled their clothes.

Laughing decades later, she said she could have kept each one in a shoe box.

Back then, infant ID bracelets were unknown. Infant footprints were unknown. That caused the trouble. They were named Arthur and Walter. They grew. The family moved temporarily into a house on Walsh Street in San Antonio, within a block of his family town-house and close enough to Five Points and John Fest Store, where they did all their shopping for medicines.

Later (some said a year), despite all her precautions, one died. The problem was which?

Lena said it was one; George "knew" it was the other. Impasse. Neither would yield. There had never been an Arthur or a Walter in the family on either side. Their children (the twin's siblings) later speculated that each had named one for whatever reason, and wanted it to be the survivor. Appearances may not have been considered.

They reached a compromise. They agreed to name the survivor John, reason unknown. They moved back to the country, to the "Miller Place," where they started a small dairy, and John could have a ready supply of milk, cream, cottage cheese, and cream gravies. He prospered.

The story of which twin was too good to keep. At Locke Hill School his siblings—and John—spread the word. Everybody heard it. He heard: Who are you really? Maybe the other one survived. Which one do you think you are? Who *are* you?

One version from Frank Bluemel the elder wondered (to his face) if John had only half a brain. John's sister, Alice, said that he had twice as much brain—he could think up mischief fast enough for two.

Who can tell how deeply the loss of an identical twin (of any age) embeds itself in the survivor? For the rest of his life, whenever anybody mentioned his twin, John wouldn't answer, but he'd get thoughtful, as if listening.

WAYFARING STRANGERS

Nobody knew where they were coming from. Nobody ever knew where they were going. They came outbound between Helotes and San Geronimo.

He told the people who came to help that his wife had taken sick suddenly and died and was buried "back there a ways." He had helped strangers bury her.

He was sick, too. That's why he stopped. He was evidently on his way either to West Texas (and California?) or to Mexico via Eagle Pass—the road led to both. He was too sick to tell them anything useful—he kept things to himself, expecting to recover.

In the wagon with the few family belongings were two little blonde, blue-eyed girls. They were too young to tell their names.

The man died very soon after arriving. He was buried immediately (something contagious?) under a big tree, thus becoming the first burial in what became the Trevino family cemetery. But over the years the site of the grave has been lost. He is there but nobody can say for sure where he is.

Some papers he had with very little money gave the name, Whittaker. One version uses Whiteacre. No first name survives. And nobody can say what happened to those papers.

The two little girls were taken in (adopted unofficially) by the Torres family, to raise with their own. One was given the name Dolores (Sorrows); the other, Soledad (Solitude), Lola and Soley.

When they were grown, they married two Cadena brothers, who had connections with Monclova, Mexico, family, or with commercial connections—they were cloth wholesalers. Lola settled on what is now Skyhawk Drive (formerly Hausman Road). Soley settled on (old) Prue Road, roughly a mile away.

In life they were not separated.

But there is no report, Torres or Cadena, that either of them ever tried to find their father's grave.

Most people, uninformed, simply thought of them as the blonde Torres girls.

There is a sobering possibility. There was a small Cadena cemetery just north of the Cadena house. As late as the 1950s it was still there, set into a semicircle of trees. There were plain wooden crosses with the names obliterated by time and weather. One grave had a broken baby bed on it. It is possible that, lacking documentation, one or both of the sisters (and husbands?) were buried there. Older Cadena family used to go visit the cemetery on All Souls Day. They knew what we don't.

Worse, when Loop 1604 was cut through the area, all landmarks changed. The graves may be under the 1604 access road as it approaches Hausman Road.

But the Torres family has reunions and the Cadena descendants are invited.

CHARCOAL CITY

Charcoal City was not a city. It was a wide band in an arc from, roughly, Median Lake before the lake was there to New Braunfels. (There is a book, *Charcoal City*, by Fritz and Emily Toepperwein, from their Highlands Press, 1950, in Boerne, Texas. It is out-of-print and pricey.)

Before and during The Depression cedar chopping and charcoaling were low-end income producers. Clearing the land of the parasitic cedar helped the land. There were a great many more choppers than charcoalers. The system for most landowners was chop and burn.

Bandera Road and Scenic Loop Road had choppers working.

Charcoaling used cedar trunks and heavy limbs. The rest of each tree fell as natural mulch to help the soil. There were several kinds of charcoaling, but one was most popular. The cedar was piled into a man-high mound and then (with more back-breaking drudgery) covered with several inches of dirt. The pile was set afire with kindling at the base. The fire smoldered for days. The only danger was rain.

After the fire had burned out, the charcoal was dug out of the dirt and put into sacks for sale.

Chopping and charcoaling never paid much, and choppers had the reputation of being the roughest, toughest people to be found in any job. It was a Spartan living.

The oldest Marnock son, Alfred, was a charcoaler before he married. His place of operation was on top of a hill behind the Marnock house. Better winds, he said.

World War II destroyed Charcoal City. It took all the men for "service" or for support labor, at Camp Stanley for instance, which had ex-choppers in the manual labor areas. They were glad to get better pay. The lowest wages at "Stanley" were rich compared with chopping.

Side-note: the odor of burning cedar is indescribable and unforgettable. Depending on the winds, people throughout the Settlement knew for certain when somebody was charcoaling.

CAVE DWELLERS

The Settlement area is riddled with caves, mostly nondescript but some with names (Roberts' Cava, a.k.a., Robbers Cave) or with scientific value.

Dr. Marnock, an amateur "snake scientist," found a new species of non-venomous snake outside a now unidentified cave, and recognized that it was a new species. That species has been named for him.

But the folklore-glamorous cave is the Madla Cave off Scenic Loop Road. Depending on the discussion, it is home to a special lizard or to a special cricket. Both versions are true.

The lizard is albino and blind, and probably unique to that cave. Almost nobody has ever actually seen one, but everybody knows about them—San Antonio, UT/Austin, the curious. They may be endangered.

The other inhabitant is an albino cricket—some say it is transparent—which is eyeless. It too may be endangered.

But the stories live on. The last time I heard them mentioned was at lunch at the Olde Towne Grille (the Old Rock Store, Maud's). Two-old timers brought them up when one saw a "good luck cricket" on the concrete porch while he was coming in.

But there is a taboo cave near the Madla Cave. On the Lee Ranch a nameless cave with a spring-fed creeklet has a sinister (testimonial) reputation. It is only a cavity under a limestone ledge (be careful!) where it is home to (or a breeding colony for) venomous snakes, specifically Cottonmouths and Coral Snakes. Mark Bacon, who had rented (perhaps) the Ranch one summer, invited his folks and their folks to come paddle or wade in the little creek.

He went a day or two early to clean up the area if necessary. He felt something hit his shoe. A Coral Snake had missed his shoe top by a couple of inches and had struck his rubber heel. He killed it.

Then he got sick.

When he got home, he called off the gathering.

SEABIRDS

Charco Martinez, known as The Lagoon by both Woller families, occupied an area east of Frank Woller Road, west of Babcock, and south of Hausman. A petro-geologist living nearby during the 1950s and '60s said it was 10,000 to 50,000 years old, and possibly a great deal older.

It was fed from the east by two creeks when they overflowed so that it did not stagnate. It was home to insects (ah, fireflies!), birds, critters, and deer. It was an away-from-home source of water for Joe Woller's cows.

But it also served as home to migrating seabirds.

The Charco overflow creek crossed the dirt road to its west, creating a bog for vehicles, buggies and, later, cars and wagons. The Charco creek crossed the upper fields of the Frank Woller property. It then turned southwestward through the Benke-Naegelin property.

Nobody could say when the seabirds first came, but the site was part of their migration pattern.

And when they arrived at the Charco creek twice a year, it was sometimes not noticed at first. When the fields had corn, milo maize, or oats, the resting birds were not easily seen. But when the fields were rented to Kenneth Evers for grazing, the creek and its visitors could be seen—and photographed by locals and tourists.

They were Cattle Egrets, comfortable with cows. They have no natural predators in their migrations. So, as wildlife, they seemed fearless. A photographer could approach within three or four feet before they would flutter an additional two or three feet away.

On each visit the tall, elegant white birds would stay two or three days and then leave as simply as they came.

Then came the developers of Hunters Chase. Taking advantage of a once-in-a-century drought, the developers had the Charco declared dry land instead of its "permanent" wetlands. History be damned, now is now. The developers blocked the overflow end, reversing the flow, so that the "little creek" had to flow backward into the two eastern creeks that had fed it.

The Charco creek dried up.

The Egrets came as always but found no sustaining creeklet. They left the next day. On the return migration, the Egrets came again, and again found the area dry. The next day they were gone, a loss along with the Charco, an old-timer said.

But Jimmy Moos, over by Galm Road, reported that the Egrets started coming to a small wet tributary of the Helotes Creek.

Not gone. No grave damage to migrations. Just displaced.

CHEWING TOBACCO

[Note: This tale comes from the overlap of the Helotes Settlement and the Shavano Settlement. One of the four people lived and worked in the Helotes Settlement the rest of his life.]

The Adams family lived in a house tucked away at the end of a gravel road, slightly diagonal to the Fredericksburg Road. Their neighbors back there were Warren and Mary Hull, with their two daughters, one a ballerina.

Papa and Mama Adams had two sons, Albert and another, who was retarded. Albert was normal. The other could dress himself, wash, and eat. But, best of all, he was trained from the time they accepted that he was "not right" to do as he was told. No exceptions.

Papa Adams developed throat cancer. By the time anyone outside the family knew it, he was chewing tobacco constantly. And swallowing the juice. It numbed the pain, he said.

Of course he got worse, was easily tired, then tired all the time, then partly bedridden, and finally totally bed-ridden. Mama and Albert did what they could and the other, doing what he could, helped out. Papa became thin and too weak to sit up. He couldn't feed himself. But he chewed tobacco.

One Saturday morning Mama and Albert went to get groceries and tobacco at Bluemel's Store, the closest available. The other was told to sit and watch Papa.

When they got back, Papa was dead with a gun beside him. The other one was sitting there, watching him.

They figured that Papa had told his son to go get the gun, and then told him how to get the ammunition and bring it (versions vary: shotgun or rifle?). Then he had to explain how to load the gun. And, weak as he was, he had to tell his son how to pull or push the trigger. And then he must have told his son to sit and wait for Mama. All of that happened in the hour or so they were gone. Evidently Papa had been planning it.

Stories exploded. Papa had fired the gun, they said, but nobody could explain how he got it and loaded it with ammunition from another room. Someone suggested that "someone else" had done it, with the Other One serving as a convenient scapegoat, untouchable legally. But who else? And why? A mercy killing? Another wondered whether Papa was dead before Mama and Albert left. Did they know what Papa was planning? Trying to get information from the Other was pointless.

The stories flashed through both settlements. Everybody heard a version. Everybody had a private solution. But the central fact fascinated everyone: how could a helpless man do that?

Of course, the Other One was unable to tell them anything they could use. He didn't know. He didn't remember. He did what he was told. They came to believe that he actually didn't know what he was doing or what he had done. His brain did not perceive a sequence.

The Sheriff ruled that it was unassisted suicide. Case closed.

But not entirely. For decades, at least for a generation, somebody could bring it up and get lively opinionated discussion started.

A common trigger of the reminiscences was seeing someone chewing tobacco.

THE NATURAL CURE

It doesn't take much to start a Settlement rumor or initiate a legend about which people other than friends were too polite to ask. So it became a mystery.

Annie Ahrens Benke, Mrs. Sam, had a brother, a veteran of World War I. He became ill. Some said it was from having been gassed in the War, but others guessed that he had come down with T.B.

Mr. Ahrens (locally: Arnz) was ordered to bed rest, fresh air, and sunshine. That was standard treatment for T.B.

Annie and Sam set up a stout tent on the west, sunny, side of their house. Word spread that it had a kerosene stove for cold weather.

Annie or her children, Verna Belle (now Steubing) and Raymond, took his meals to him three times a day—no special diet, just what they were having. Well, also citrus, lots of citrus.

In time, neighbors passing by forgot that he was there. Strangers passing by, most likely couldn't see the tent.

If he was mentioned, it was with approval. The tent treatment was certainly better than being in Legion, Texas, just east of Kerrville. Legion was a veterans' hospital, a hideous box-like dead-end hospital for "lung" patients.

It may be odd, but nobody remembers clearly when he came to the tent, and even more strangely, nobody can say when he left.

He was there. Then he wasn't.

Area people never heard whether he got well and left, or was transferred to Legion, or whether he died there.

It was reported later by a friend and neighbor that Annie Benke confided one day that she had lost her oldest son, Gene, and felt that helping her brother somehow made her feel easier.

But the family never talked about it or never gave any details, any information about the man in the tent.

BIRD-BOY

There was a semi-legendary (gossip) human being everybody had heard of but few had ever seen, Shelley Lee of the Lee Ranch above the Scenic Loop Playground.

Unless someone visited the ranch, there was little chance of seeing him. Shelley was a hunchback with a "pigeon breast." Otherwise he was healthy, active, bright. To shield him from potentially hurtful comment, the Lees kept him home (not unusual—many families kept even sound kids home).

Shelley loved company. Kids are far more accepting and quicker than adults, after an initial encounter. Area kids asked to go visit him.

Kids being kids, it could have happened to any of them, to anybody. But since it was Shelley the legend was nourished and spread.

One day the kids were discussing birds: what bird would you like to be? Shelley told them that he had always wanted to fly. Of course sooner or later all boys do. Someone came up with the idea that they would help him. He was delighted.

They got him up on the top of the hay barn, the highest point. They gave him two turkey wings (one version

says they were buzzard wings). They told him to flap them to fly or hold them steady to glide.

Eagerly and unafraid, he jumped. He flapped strenuously. And, of course, he fell straight down, ten or more feet.

The kids panicked.

But luckily he didn't break anything. Maybe it was fear of punishment, but the fall scared some sense into them. Their play changed.

But Shelley was a hero to all of them, and to anyone who heard of it. Adults were amazed and relieved.

He was the only one who was ever brave enough to jump off a barn, trying to fly. The unintended victim became a Hero.

EDWARDS FLAT

It was talked about in the Settlement, but most knew it only by report. Edwards Flat was east of the Leon Creek and west of Fredericksburg Road. It could be seen from the Leon bluffs. But it was surrounded by scrub brush, young mesquites and the like, with a dirt road with a "gap" entrance that swerved a little to keep the idly curious from looking in.

Some Saturdays and/or Sundays young men (no mention of females, not even girlfriends or mothers) gathered for games of "work-up" baseball if they didn't have enough on hand for teams. If they had teams they were random, not partisan.

Sometimes there were horseraces. The track was a wide circle around the baseball field.

There may have been some betting among the spectators, but the real betting was between the racers. Frank Woller the younger ran his new pony, Dago. He never admitted it, but Dago never won (or he'd have bragged about it).

When World War I came, Frank and his horseracing-baseball chums, Jimmy Logan and Christian Evers, went into the army together, at Fort Sam and stayed there till the war was over.

Edwards Flat did not survive the war.

When they came back, Edwards Flat did not or could not start up again. It yielded to cedar and mesquite.

Long after that, in the tale-telling phase, while he was working at Camp Stanley, I wondered out loud why he had not raced Daisy instead of Dago. Not broken for riding, he said.

Edwards Flat has never been found on any map.

DAISY AND THE STORK—

Once her children were old enough to be left alone for a day or two, Mary Woller served as a midwife in the Settlement. She delivered all the Lieba children born before 1925—in the Lieba home on Huebner Road, one parcel west of the Locke Hill Cemetery.

When she was summoned (by unknown means) she had her kids back Daisy between the shafts of her light two-wheeler. She packed her special scissors and left. Everyone at home was fatalistic. Nobody could predict any trip with Daisy.

Daisy was lean and fast, but she was the most easily spooked horse anyone knew of. A piece of paper fluttering beside the road was enough to make her either stop dead and refuse to move or run away. She might do both in one trip.

If she stopped, the driver had to get down and lead her by the bridle past the trouble spot. If she ran away she would not respond to commands or restraints. The driver had to ride it out, spending energy to keep the two-wheeler from turning over. Mary could do that. Her children didn't dare try.

One of the problems with Daisy was that sometimes she imagined a spook. There was no sitting back—she required constant attention.

Evidently Mary was good at her job. She had more requests than she could handle.

Her son Frank said that she was proud that she had never lost a baby or a mother, although she had handled some "difficult" cases, breach births.

According to Frank she always had a girl's name or a boy's name ready.

She reported that nobody ever considered Daisy.

THE INDIAN TREE

Off to the left of the Scenic Loop Road (What was its name before the Scenic Loop Playground was established?) in a field there still stands a big oak tree. There are two stories about it. Indian stories.

In one, "the men" left to work somewhere nearby, leaving the woman alone but armed. When her husband came home, he found the crime. She had been raped and hanged by Indians.

The other story says that she was raped by Indians and hanged herself.

Either way (with a woman alone, Indians, rape, her death), it was the last reported Indian event in the Settlement.

THE MOELLER-MARNOCK SHOOTOUT

(Marnock version)

[SPOILER ALERT: This is the Marnock family version. For the objective, documented one, see Cynthia Massey's writings; she is the historian-reporter. This is a folktale.]

The county or state decided to survey a line from Culebra Road to Helotes along what is now FM 1560, crossing Moeller's property and passing his house. Moeller objected.

Dr. Marnock had a government contract that included right-of-way, and he had the equipment. He came northward with a helper.

Moeller confronted him, ordered him off the property. Then he threatened: if Marnock came back, he'd get his gun and kill him. The helper was a witness.

Undaunted, Marnock came back with his equipment, his helper, his papers—the contract—and a surveyor's license. He also brought a gun.

Moeller was outraged. Marnock tried to present his credentials. Moeller waved them aside. Moeller raised his gun, but Marnock was ready and faster.

He killed Moeller. The helper went into Helotes to get help.

Murder or self-defense?

There were trials in San Antonio, with hung juries. After some time, the charges were dropped (credible witness lacking, or just ignored).

The surveying was completed as planned.

But those trials. . . . Were they vindication or injustice?

THE CULVERT

During Prohibition, Helotes Settlement men laughed about the halfway mark between the Catholic Church, Los Reyes, and Zion Lutheran Church.

It was a culvert on what is now Riggs Road near the (much newer, relocated) Catholic Church. A moonshiner would leave bottles of hooch in the upstream side of the culvert. On an unviolated honor system, customers would take a bottle and leave the payment ($1) in a gallon bucket. Lutheran and Catholic men were ecumenical at that spot. It was too important for anyone to cheat.

Men from Riggs' (Helotes) Dance Hall were the best customers.

THE DEVIL IN THE OUTHOUSE

[Note: This tale did not originate in the Settlement. There are versions all over the Hispanic Southwest. San Antonio has several, including the La Gloria with its rooftop dance floor, and others. Artell Dorman, researching for a paper at the Texas Forklore Society (on another subject), found a version in Ojinaga, Mexico—but that devil had a chicken foot. But she didn't find this one. Why not? This one was imported and localized. (Who knows why?)]

The Settlement residents were dancers. They had dances at or near what is now Villarreal's, Riggs' (Helotes) Dance Hall, Braun Hall, and Tutsin's Dance Hall on Culebra Road—sometimes called "The Culebra" by old-timers.

One night a handsome stranger came to Tutsin's. People supposed he was from San Antonio. He was the best-dressed man at the dance. Everyone was cordial. He was courtly in behavior.

He asked permission of chaperones or dancing partners and then danced with all the pretty young women. They said he was an excellent dancer.

But during a Paul Jones one of the older women looked down, pointed at his foot and screamed. The music stopped. Other women screamed. The elegant stranger broke through some onlookers and ran out of the dance hall and into the men's outhouse. The men gathered around it, demanding that he come out.

While they were waiting, he came out of the women's outhouse behind them. They forced the door of the men's outhouse. He wasn't there. When they turned they saw him disappear in a flash of light and a puff of smoke.

The stranger with the goat hoof (the "Cloven Hoof") had escaped. The dance started up again and nobody was alarmed by the event.

Strangely, no eyewitness ever reported it. The story came from a man "who knew a man who. . . ." The story is always at two or three removes from the teller, of course.

A major question is, Who imported it? A second is, Why? And another: Why localize and not just tell it the way he had heard it?

One old-timer commented, on hearing it at El Chapparal Restaurant, "That would never happen at the Helotes Dance Hall."

THE TROPHY BUCK

[In memoriam, Bill Cockrell, who cried telling it.]

The CCC gangs, involved with clearing away brush and trees for the widening of Bandera Road beyond Helotes, told and retold this story and marveled at it.

They lived in a camp and unofficially supplemented their standard rations with squirrels and rabbits they shot. The sound of gunfire was common.

One ordinary evening they gathered after work. The cook had the cook-fire burning. Into the middle of the camp came a magnificent buck, a trophy. With him was a skinny doe, with her cheek against his flank. She had been badly damaged, too thin, blind. He had led her to water and to food, but she couldn't see it and didn't eat much.

When they stopped to see what was going on, he suddenly whirled away from her, jumped away from them, and ran out of sight in the early darkness.

The men didn't know what to do. He couldn't take care of her any more. They couldn't either, but he had brought her to them.

One of them decided to do what they were all thinking. With one shot he killed her.

Another of the men told them that the buck had come back to a short distance behind them and watched what they did.

Then with a kind of natural majesty he slowly turned, first offering a full profile (a hunter's dream), and then slowly walked away. He had done what he came to do. He had brought her with a purpose. The men had understood and had done what was necessary, what he could not do. He was satisfied.

But for a few days, someone or other reported hearing him snuffling in the brush nearby.

The men made decisions. The younger ones tried to learn the landmarks so they could come back next deer season.

But the older ones decided that they would not hunt in that area again.

NOMAD

There are about as many versions of this tale as there are tellers. Tales and speculations have swirled around him for decades.

One says he came from Dallas where he was a sleek, clean-shaven DJ with a conventional haircut, all slicked down. Others add that he claimed to be a cousin of Ozzie Nelson. Not true.

Another says he was a scrawny orphan with a bad complexion (hence the beard) who wandered about with his acoustic guitar, singing for contributions.

Many if not most tie him to John Floore's Country Store in its second, current location, now with a dance hall and stage added. His connection started in John Floore's time.

They say that Floore practically adopted him by giving him a cot to the left of the doorway behind the bar counter. That "room" was his anytime he wanted it, come and go.

What he did during the week they don't say. But on Sunday afternoons, later evenings, he entertained the customers. It was a family show with grandparents and kids. They loved him and kept coming back. He was a crowd builder and Floore appreciated it.

Later, when Floore's dance/concerts got underway, he was a familiar figure, dancing with all the pretty young girls. "He was cute but a grungy one," says one now mature woman. "He danced with all of us. He was persistent."

Then he started getting bookings away from Helotes: Leon Springs and Bandera. But he always came back to do shows for Floore's, even after Joe Algueseva became the long-term proprietor. It was his way of paying back to Floore's what he felt he owed. All the locals would fill up the space.

Even after he became famous, a "name" with a band, a tour bus, recordings, and sometimes tabloid controversial behavior, he came back, sometimes unannounced. He did benefits for farmers. He had tax problems. People loved him.

And Helotes "regulars" felt that "he was ours. We knew him when. . . . We knew him first."

He has a bigger name now than all of the other Floore's performers, maybe than all of them combined.

Still grungy (costume or mask?), campaigning for marijuana and being arrested for possession and having his tour bus impounded, or being indicted for millions in delinquent taxes, there is still his loyalty to his origins that people talk about and admire. All along he has made music. Now he also makes news.

But in Helotes he is still "our Willie Nelson."

INDIAN MIDDENS AND GRAVES

There is enough Indian lore in the Settlement to fill a book: stolen horses, murder, rapes, smoke signals (always way over there), kidnapped pre-teen boys (to replenish the battle losses). On still afternoons, on front porches there were stories of Indian cave hideouts (always long before and not here) and Indian campsites, like the famous one near Kreuzberg east of Boerne, believed to be the source of all flint and chert "points."

But nobody ever mentioned that there were no stories or reports of Indian burials. They took their dead with them? Where? "In one of those caves," Hugo said.

Well, yes, later a hunch-backed Indian skeleton was recovered beside the Salado Creek, south of where it now crosses Loop 410. He had to be a hereditary chief or a chief's son to grow to maturity. Indians destroyed the crippled and the ill. It was too much trouble to take them along. But that burial was way over there north of San Antonio, anyway.

Even their campsites were rare finds. Their fires were put out, usually with dirt, and the stones of the fire circle were kicked away. There were no ceramics or pottery left behind, if they had any. They roasted everything. And they were constantly mobile.

So when Archie Gerfers, son of John Gerfers, who owned the land, found an Indian campsite, he didn't celebrate or brag about it.

It was atop a bluff overlooking the Leon Creek. It was on a natural triangle of land. The other side dropped to the dry bed of a long-dead tributary.

Helena Gerfers Igo reported that well into her teens or even later (she remembered the post-Krakatoa sunsets), the Leon ran year round, with minnows, perch, turtles, and even crawfish. Regional birds watered there. So did critters and deer.

The site was a natural lookout with a full view of the plain from the dog-leg curving Leon to the hill with the (later) De Zavala Road on it.

According to Archie, there was abundant evidence that the site was in use: arrowheads, scrapers for preparing deer hides for leather or rawhide, bird sticks for capturing birds.

When his nephew, Totsy (George) Gaubatz, John Fox, and I were about twelve years old, Archie decided we were mature enough to see a "sacred" Indian site. He believed that the site included a burial when it was being abandoned. He made us promise solemnly. John Fox did the Scout Oath, repeating after Archie, that we would never reveal the location.

He led us there, up treacherous paths. When we got there, he lectured us about our responsibility. Then he told us we could "scuff" up one memorial piece. (He did not call them souvenirs.)

He showed us how: with the edge of a shoe sole or the tip of the shoe sole—no sticks or implements, because they could damage deeper. We turned up arrowheads. Mine was about two inches long. I forget what theirs were. We received another lecture on the sacredness of the place. "Notice that there are no bushes or weeds." That was, somehow, a clincher.

Johnny Gaubatz and David Fox pestered their older brothers uselessly.

Then across the years, Archie died after moving to Boerne. Then Totsy, a U.S. Border Ranger, died, and then John Fox, the ex-West Point faculty member, who died of a fall while touring Russia. He left behind a book, with no mention of Indians. That left me, with the solemn promise, responsibility, respect for sacred places, and encroaching developers. The John Gerfers estate was sold by his widow, Ella Eckert Gerfers, to "Mr. Delavan" for a housing development, Dell Oaks.

I did not want desecration.

The rest of the story is unhappy, even now, years later.

I went for walks in the woods. I dropped pebbles into the Leon when it was running under the culvert on Hausman Road. I did not even try to revisit the site.

Then I called the Archaeology Department at UTSA to ask advice on where to go with information about an untouched site. That was a brick wall: not interested, since I am not a professional archaeologist. "How do you know it isn't just an abandoned picnic site?"

I then called the Anthropology Department at UTSA. I found another brick wall, since I am not a professional anthropologist. "We have collected all the samples we need." There was no interest in an unviolated site. "If we ever need it, we have ways of finding it." Scornful.

With that reception, I decided—right or wrong—that full obliteration would be better than "going public" and opening it up to the merely curious or, worse, artifact dealers found at gun shows, rock shows, and hobby shows.

The bulldozers came and scraped the area clean; the machines could be seen from Hausman Road. They pushed the "trash" into the Leon or into the dry tributary.

A house sits up there now. Apparently, the site has become greenspace.

The house has a view of the plain from the dog-leg Leon and the Edwards Flat to its east (where there were horseraces on some Sundays and adult baseball other Sundays. Frank Woller the younger played there). The view included the bluff paralleling De Zavala Road.

Guilt. The destruction of the site has weighed heavily on me ever since—did I do enough? I never visited the scrapings.

[Sidenote: The site was only a short walk from the house, where decades earlier, Cleto panicked about Indians.]

FOOLS' GOLD

From its beginning the Settlement was honeycombed with lost money, hidden money, buried gold, ambiguous directions (Which cave was that?). Some was hidden by a dying stagecoach driver, under attack. Some was under a hearthstone. Some was guarded by a phantom. They were tantalizing tales, inviting, all of them.

So, when Alice Igo Bowman found an "Indian" mark on a good-sized oak in a pasture her husband Henry rented from the three De Zavalas (Adina was spokesman), buried money was the only possible explanation.

The mark was a long arrow, pointing downward, gouged into the bark long before, long enough that it had "healed" and was growing over. She may have told Henry—we don't know—but she did tell her sister-in-law, Annie Woller Igo. They conspired. The tree was "out there" in the woodlands, but nobody could have found it easily (or at all), except those two.

One day while the kids were away and Henry was on his daily milk run to Metzger's Dairy, Alice and Annie with a pick and shovel, a grubbing hoe, work gloves, straw hats, and a jug of water wrapped in wet burlap went to find out.

They dug a hole roughly five by five feet. The soil was "easy," a good sign. They believed that the easy soil was refill, put back in to cover something.

Indians? But what would nomadic Indians, hunters and gatherers, expect, burying gold? ("Something" had become "gold.") They dug on, planning.

Then, while they were stooped over in the pit, they found some U.S. coins, fairly recent ones. Annie said, "Alice, don't move." (That was a universal warning about rattlesnakes.) "But look at the foot of the tree." There were two work shoes and the bottoms of workpants. "Alice, you know what we have to do." With one mind each grabbed an ankle and tugged hard. "Uncle" Joe Gerfers, Lena's oldest brother, crashed down onto his bottom. They said that if he had any more of "their" coins in his pockets, they would have to tickle him till he gave up. It was only a threat, but he emptied his pocket of some change. And dropped it into the pit.

By then they were laughing so hard they cried. He was the tribe's jester and loved what he had done to them. Alice and Annie, depleted by the work and the laughing, had to be helped out of the pit. The two kept all the money even though he wanted it back. They left the pit for Henry's dairy workmen to fill in.

To sustain their story, they agreed on a plan. Yes, they had found money. No, they wouldn't say what kind or how much. Gold? No answer. To his delight, they included Uncle Joe (uncle to Alice and Annie's husband) in their repeated tale, as a chance witness. And they spread the story. And the story spread all on its own, through families, extended families, neighbors, and friends. Soon enough people were roaming through the woodlands, looking at tree trunks. Uncle Joe wanted to "fix" several more trees but didn't.

The original tree with the filled pit became a visitors' destination. Harris Bowman, Alice's son, would take guests to it. Con-man blood was jigging in him. He would take the curious on an elaborately complicated path to the tree, and warn them not to step on the filling-in dirt. Then he would lead them around another complicated way till they reached De Zavala Road and then home. Everybody was satisfied.

Then Henry, a master deadpan, did his own prank. He asked what if they had stopped too soon, just inches away, and the money was still there.

"But we got all the money," one would say, "and we have Uncle Joe as our witness." And they grinned.

But Alice and Annie wondered if they could get the dairy hands to reopen the pit. No, leave it alone, the way it is.

The tree with all the others was bulldozed to prepare for a strip center. Luckily, except for Harris, they had all died. So nobody ever knew any more about that sign.

Earth keeps its secrets.

THE SKELETON HOUSE

For decades, even generations, the Skeleton House stirred curiosity. It was there for a century, more or less. It was an almost square house made of caliche (cut and cured in blocks) and flagstone, with thick walls and windows with thick lumber finishing. There were no floors. Toward the end there was a ten-foot tree growing out of one of the rooms. The empty doors opened east and west.

It stood in the right-angle bend of Babcock Road, across from a squadron of early Settlement mailboxes.

It was built by Theodore (Teddo) Benke, who assumed that his wife, Piercy Michelson, had inherited the land. For some reason he checked the deed. He was shocked and outraged to learn that the elder Michelsons had left the property to Alex Benke, Teddo's oldest son. They evidently thought that Teddo might sell it.

Work stopped immediately and permanently.

He built a large wooden house next door (by yards). It remained unpainted always. The central room was a large open space, with a scattering of beds. There was an outside small bedroom for the older boys, Alex and Laurie. There was west of the house a bunkhouse for hired help, if any.

Folks heard that there were legal challenges to the deed. The two houses were razed, along with a softstone bathroom Piercy had had constructed from the walls of an old house a half-mile on the other side of the Leon Creek. She demolished a century-old historical landmark they had been using to store hay bales.

A gasoline service station stands approximately where the Skeleton House stood. The concrete underground rainwater cistern is lost to history, filled in, of course. But its appealing echoes of childhood calls were gone before the Skeleton House fell.

PHANTOM CEMETERY

Frank Naegelin from Castroville was in General Black-Jack Pershing's army along the Rio Grande, fighting Pancho Villa's forces. He was asleep in a sleeping bag across the river between Laredo and Eagle Pass when a bullet hit him. He had his arm curled over his head. The bullet hit the elbow and left his bent hand at the wrist; or vice versa. It wrecked the usefulness of that arm and got him a medical discharge, a medal, and a 100% disability pension.

He married Dora Benke and moved to the Benke compound. The government decided, evidently that the small pension was not enough to provide food, shelter, and clothing, with no other income.

The government decided to give him a source of income. He was given a profession along with all its necessities. He received multiple beehives, bee colonies, equipment to extract honey from the combs, bee nets for protection, gloves and hats, glass jars with lids, and a stipend for a while until he developed an income.

The bee colony was within easy range of the Huajilla shrubs (a.k.a., White Brush), whose flowers produced a superior honey. The business grew. The family helped.

The white hives were placed, spaced evenly, on the upper slope of Benke's main field, close to Frank Woller's cattle tank (bees need water) and just south of the grave of Edwin Benke who died young, age twelve more or less. Edwin's grave was unmarked, but we know where he is; anyone taking the trail from the John Igo House to the Naegelin House, passed just a couple of yards from it. The spot was distinguished by having a ground ivy cover, the only ground ivy in the area.

From the lower field or across the Woller fields, the hives looked like a private cemetery with orderly, uniform gravestones. Folks who didn't know it was bees assumed it was a private Benke cemetery backed against a wide stand of oaks.

It became a phantom cemetery.

From the Naegelin gate on Hausman Road (the new Skyhawk Drive) there was no cemetery to be seen. A slight rise in the center of the field hid the "tombstones."

When Frank and Dora died, the land was parceled out to three daughters. Ultimately, the compound and the fields were sold to a developer, who sold it to NISD for the Brandeis High School. Unless Mildred Naegelin Babcock signed the papers to have his grave moved, Edwin was plowed under.

The bee hives were neglected after Frank's death. And really did disappear. Maybe the bulldozers and graders knocked down what was left.

And the world is a sadder place without the Huajilla honey.

CISTERNS?

When the U.S. Government put in what neighbors called the Radar Tower, the top of the hill was cleared of scrub brush. The hill, north of the old Joe Woller house (now an Historical Landmark), south of the Benke compound, had twin mysteries revealed. There, near the western edge of the bluff, were two shafts or holes, a yard or more in diameter about eight feet deep. They were lined with stones. Two cisterns? Then someone discovered at the bottom of one a hole parallel to the surface, the "size of a man's leg."

That undid the cistern theory. If not lined cisterns, then what? The Joe Woller family reported that they had no knowledge of them.

Pre-Woller (1876)? Of course Indians must have done it. But the Comanches, the Apaches and others were not builders. They were hunters and gatherers.

Pre-1876, but not Indians. Earlier settlers who left no other discovered trace.

By coincidence a member of the Frank Woller family remembered that his uncle, Alfred Marnock, had been a charcoal burner in the 19th century. Marnock did dirt-mound firing. But had talked about the necessity of air for flames, to feed the burning.

Bingo!

Logs stood upright in the "cisterns" and capped with earth would burn since the holes at the bottom served as flues.

The stones looked smudged (soot?) but weathered.

A few years earlier three "wells" were also found just north of the (old) Lock Hill School, when the WPA workers were looking for field stones to build the Lock Hill Auditorium. They reported three "wells" roughly the size, shape, and depth of those in the Settlement. They were also lined with stones. They were on top of the hill, on top of a bluff, but close to the edge, a curious place for dug water wells.

The cisterns in the Woller property became a destination for Sunday walks. Friends were taken there.

Developers moved in and scraped the top of the hill for building. They also scraped away an old, unmarked family cemetery.

When they were through, the cisterns were gone.

But nobody has explained why settlers would stay long enough to want and build charcoal burners and then leave without any other trace.

THE WOLF MAN

At the end of a dirt road at an acute angle off Bandera Road at or near French Creek was the Wolf Man's unpainted cabin. It was always dark. Nobody ever reported a light there.

It contained a coal-oil two-burner table-top stove, some shelves with supplies, a large box or chest, a work-table, and a chair. And in a corner there was a pile of wolf pelts. Wolf only—Frank Woller the younger visited him to ask if he was interested in other pelts. No.

The Wolf Man was lean and sinewy, sun or wind browned. He spoke little. But it was known that he had a license or certificate or government contract to hunt wolves for a bounty. Wolves had not been a problem in the Settlement or an extended area around it, not for years. Old-timers told stories they had heard of even earlier times.

But the Wolf Man managed.

Stories arose. He could see in the dark. He could walk in the woods or anywhere without making a sound. He could howl like a wolf. He ate meat only, half-raw.

Yet there he was.

Some landowners reported now and then that their German Shepherds had disappeared. “Killed by wolves,” the bounty hunter said. Oddly, the “dead” Shepherds’ bodies were never found. “Kidnapped by ranchers, then,” he said.

Even more oddly, other breeds were not attacked: hounds, coon dogs, border collies, terriers, bulldogs. Easier prey went unattacked.

After the Wolf Man left the area without warning, some farmers and ranchers got German Shepherds again. The new dogs were monitored very carefully. Months went by, but not one was attacked or kidnapped.

Farmers and ranchers would not believe that it was a coincidence.

THE BUZZARD COLONY

Buzzards are not pretty. But they attract a kind of helpless fascination. In the Settlement Turkey Vultures are called buzzards, although there were stories of other kinds.

At a bend of the Leon Creek, downstream from (Old) Prue Road, there was a large colony of them, dozens, maybe even hundreds. Their sound was deep nasal, and scary. And they hissed.

Boys, perhaps as a local rite-of-passage, felt they had to find the place and come back with specific stories of their own. They went armed with slingshots (known of course by their grosser name). Their aim was to stir up activity.

But one boy took along his uncle's single-shot "22." The other boys were uneasy, wary. It was his idea that it would be interesting and fun to kill one and watch the others eat it.

He did, and they did.

After that, trips to the Colony lost their appeal (for that generation). Even a tentative challenge to see who would bring back a buzzard egg had no takers.

Their fathers knew but did nothing to discourage the practice. The boys had to learn for themselves. Kill snakes, yes; buzzards, no.

And anyway the fathers had gone through it all a generation earlier.

THE RUSTLER

Celestino was half-Indian, an imposing figure, with what became a legendary practice of law-and-order. He was his work ethic.

And having worked his way up, he became the ranch manager at Callaghan Ranch, which had a gate across the road from his house. He made it his business to be on call at any time. No one has ever reported that he took a vacation that took him away from home. He was manager of the cattle operation. Someone else managed the paperwork, the buildings, business, and the like. His word was law. Management backed him absolutely. His version was *the* version. He hired and fired cattle help without question. He carried a gun.

He noticed that fewer cattle were coming in for food and water and the salt-lick. Unalarmed, he "went looking for strays." At the far gate on the other road (Culebra?) he found lots of cattle tracks but no cattle. He understood: rustlers. He couldn't report it because, he figured, it had to be an inside job, a current cowhand or a former one.

He went back several times looking for strays. And one day he was successful. He found a cattle trailer that had two loaded, two more being loaded, and others milling around with seed corn on the ground. And two familiar men. His gun explained it all. They unloaded the cows.

He sent one back to headquarters, to report the next day as usual.

The other was his son.

He told his son to return the truck and trailer, and that he would see him later back at home.

The problem was clear: Bloodline or the law?

When the son met Celestino that evening, the Sheriff from Bandera was there. Celestino had his son arrested for rustling Callaghan's cattle. That was—then—a gravely serious charge.

The next day, Celestino paid his bail. Henry Woller, a friend of both, said later that Celestino also paid for his son's lawyer.

When the trial came, Celestino was the only prosecution witness. The son pleaded guilty; that got him a lighter sentence than a Not Guilty plea being rejected by a jury.

Under the hard stare of his father, he pledged Restitution. He received a minimum jail sentence since Celestino recommended leniency. Celestino's word was powerful wise.

When the time came Celestino and Elena drove forty or fifty miles to see their son off to prison. Elena cried. Celestino was stone-faced.

When the son returned from prison early and unannounced ("good behavior"), he had done a lot of thinking. He went to his father and knelt on one knee and asked forgiveness. Celestino put his hand on the bent head and forgave him. More tears, Elena's and the son's. Talking about it later, Celestino said it was a matter of loyalty to the son's profession. The penalty was not for rustling. It was for failing to hold to the code.

Years later, when Elena and Celestino celebrated their 70th wedding anniversary at Guadalupe Church in Helotes (they had been married at Los Reyes) the event made local history. They renewed their wedding vows in the presence of their original maid-of-honor, Mary Woller Marnock, a cousin, along with their Wedding Madrina (a custom long lost, in which the Madrina gave the wedding party the Wedding Banquet); and Frank Woller the younger, a cousin, schoolmate, and friend for eighty or more years. Someone there thought he had been the original Best Man.

This time the son served as Best Man.

SNAKES

The Settlement generated lots of snake lore.

A six-foot-long, all-green rattlesnake was killed at the Leon Creek–Hausman Road crossing.

A rattlesnake without rattles was found (good dog!) on the flat above Charco Martinez.

Two of the most productive sources of snakes remained productive even as the Settlement was shrinking. One was in a motte of middle-sized oaks at the edge of Hausman Road close to Woller Road, in what is now Bonnie Conner Park. It was a generous source of rattlers for Sam Benke, who lived across the road. He believed that they came up out of a cave.

Sam would take his hollowed-out, dried bamboo stick, about four feet long, with a rawhide thong through it to make a loop, to catch a snake and drop it into an empty sugar sack. He sold rattlers for $5 each to the Alligator Gardens and Snake Pit at the Witte Museum.

Once, he left the motte with several snakes in bags. When he got to the Witte one of the bags was empty. A rattler was loose in the car. Sam was the only one calm. He got the snake stick and prodded around until the snake buzzed. Sam re-caught it without incident.

Another generous source of snakes, of all kinds, was the Snake Place, a half-mile north of Prue Road in the Joe Woller property. It was mostly a large flat rock. It was said that nobody had ever gone there without seeing several snakes: rattlers, copperheads, corals, kings, coach whips, rat-snakes, and others. But no watersnakes. And nobody ever went there to catch snakes, not even Sam Benke. First of all, it was deep in private property. People asked permission to go there. It was an observation adventure from a car window or sometimes on foot—snake boots required. City folks in addition to relatives and friends came to shoot a snake, with pistols or 22's (short-shell only, for fear of ricochets eastward).

There have been no snake reports from there for a quarter of a century. But tales were available, like the one about the rattler that wrapped itself around a car tire, biting it, and wasn't discovered until the tire started bumping.

Dr. Marnock, an amateur herpetologist, had a collection of snake specimens in alcohol jars on shelves on the walls of his office. He treated snakebites mostly by incision and suction. And a species of snake is named for him and noted in a book, *The Snakes of Bexar County*, published by the Witte Museum. He found his snake in one of the main limestone caves between Helotes and Wagner Road, off Scenic Loop Road. It was/is non-venomous.

There are no reliable stories about what became of the bottled snakes when the house was rented out and then sold.

THE INVISIBLE BOOTLEGGER(S)

Off Hausman Road, alongside a dry feeder-creek (to the Leon) there was a producing still. Men and boys of the area knew how to find it. Some sort of code-of-honor kept them from damaging it or betraying it. Our secret . . . a brotherhood.

But nobody ever reported seeing anyone there. Ever.

Frequently, nearly daily, people at Vollmer's dairy saw a battered flatbed truck enter that property through a gap in the north fence. The truck always had a load of large sugar sacks.

People "officially" wondered what those strangers could be doing with so much sugar. Everybody knew, but nobody ever suggested that it might be bootlegging.

The women knew and gossiped about it, and it entered folklore.

When the revenuers came to the neighborhood—city folk all of them—asking questions, nobody knew anything about bootlegging. Maybe in the gravel pit in the Leon where it crossed Babcock Road?

After the revenuers left, some men went to check that the still was intact, that those treacherous revenuers had not found it and destroyed it.

The still died only when World War II rationing cut off sugar.

THE DEVIL'S SLIDE

The long, steep hill on Bandera Road going down to San Geronimo was the terror of the territory.

Wagons and carriages, coaches and buggies, "got away" and crashed or wrecked wheels. Or, with their woodblock pressure-brakes, they burned out or shattered the brakes and *then* got away.

Experienced haulers learned not to head down the road. They zigzagged as much as they could. Otherwise the weight of the vehicle pushed the mule or ox or horse. One tale tells of the "good" horse in the two-seater buggy. When the thrust became too much, the horse sat down between the shafts and was pushed, seated, all the way down to Pete Martinez's Store. The horse required a veterinarian from Pipe Creek to take care of *his* seat. It adds that the horse would not even approach the Devil's Slide after that. He would balk.

Over the years the hill was cut into, to lower the road. But accidents still happened. Nobody dared call them wrecks.

In the 1940s and maybe later, the remnants of wrecks still sat off the road. Wagons, livelihood, were salvaged.

Buggies badly damaged were left to the sun and rain and sleet. Some intact wheels were salvaged. Slowly the wreckage too disappeared.

But at last reports, the Devil's Slide is still perilous for bicycles—and skateboards?—and cars with faulty brakes. "Pump your brakes; don't hold them down."

You can't beat Mother Nature.

LOST GOLD

The stagecoach had no passengers. It had only a driver and a guard with a rifle. That meant valuable freight, usually money.

At the Leon Springs stop, at Aue's Hotel, there was an unfamiliar man watching. He took off westward on his horse while the coach was getting ready to leave—watering horses, securing extra nosebags of oats.

The coach left southward on its accustomed route.

But before the coach could reach its next station—officially Shavano, but the Linn House in practice—things went wrong. The coach came down the slope where UTSA now is. The driver or the guard decided they were being followed. Before they could climb the hill across the plain (now Regency Gardens), they were attacked. Everyone who heard of it decided, "Indians." But not necessarily. There were legendary robbers in the area (Robbers Cave is a clue).

There was shooting.

When the coach arrived at Linn House, the driver had been badly wounded and the guard was dead. But there was no freight—gold in a stout iron-bound box. The driver said the shipment was safe. He said that he and the guard had stopped momentarily slightly off-route and had hidden it in a safe place.

Of course, the station master asked him where. But he was dying. Weakly he gestured "Under," but all he said was "Easy."

Over the days, weeks, months, even years, that Under/Easy lured people to find it . . . none successfully so far as anyone knew. One consulted a fortuneteller in San Antonio. Under a bush? In an erosion gully? Standing on end in a hollow tree? Pushed in under a rock ledge?

As late as the 1960s Lena Gerfers Igo's grandson, Harris Bowman, was on occasion still searching—she owned the property (now Merrill Gardens) where the stagecoach passed. He tried a primitive metal detector. There was a brush-covered ravine that lured him—after the robbery, decades later during the Depression, that ravine had been an experimental Trench Silo for cattle food. Maybe under that?

Of course, it is possible that the robbers found it.

Easy?

Nothing so far.

THE TOTEM

On Babcock Road at the right-angle, left-elbow turn, not far from the Krempkau Divide where Babcock Road dead-ends in the Scenic Loop Road (a.k.a., "the Colorado of Texas," with a delightful echo), there stood a powerful attraction. Behind a heavy stand of brush there stood the Bull.

The brush was removed slowly or dried out, and there he stood, the primal Bull. He was about six feet tall at the shoulders and hips, about four feet wide, maybe ten feet long, with a head as formidable as a Roman battering ram.

Nobody knew who created it, or why. It seemed old. An easy opinion was that Indians (always Indians!) had left it behind—a white-man's bull, not a lean prairie one.

Over some years, visiting it became a rite of passage. Teenage males brought their girls to see it. Even the curious from San Antonio and Boerne came to see it on that not-much-travelled road. It was best seen at dusk, imposing as it was in bright sunlight. One folktale said it didn't cast a shadow. How would anyone know? It was difficult to get to, behind barbed wire fencing.

Then (when?) a trailer house was there, to its right but not close. Sometimes a lean old man was there. He was civil, but not forthcoming. No, he didn't know about it,

who did it, or why. In exchange for keeping intruders away, he had free rent for his house. He wouldn't let anyone get up onto it. He had a gun. He also had to keep it presentable, he said.

Who hired you? The owner. Who is the owner? Can't rightly say. (That's "country" for mind your own business.)

Lots of people wanted to be in a photo with it, or just to get a good shot of it. Like standing beside an elephant.

Then he'd go back to his house and his dog would set up some huge barking, as it did when he wasn't out.

That Bull stood with huge legs apart. Nothing short of an earthquake could topple it.

That idea was based on the idea that it was solid. Was it hollow, covered framework? Realistic certainly. Was that real bullhide? Filled with ground-rocks, or poured concrete (what a Herculean job that would have been!) How was it finally taken down? Who and when? Where did the pieces go?

But it disappeared. Behind new-growth brush? No. Heavy platform and all, gone. So was the truckless trailer house.

Not many years back I went looking again. I couldn't even decide where exactly it had been. The road had been "upgraded" with curves.

A recent addition to the lore is that the Bull is still there, hidden when the straight lines were cut short by the curves. But there are no new reports of sightings.

POSTAL SERVICE

The Helotes Settlement and later, Helotes, had mail service. The Post Office was for a while a wooden rack of cubbyholes at the foot of the stairs in the Marnock House. It was also for a while in the building adjoining the Rock Store (Maud Fuller's, etc.); the Postmistress was Mrs. Ross Barham.

But the colorful one was at the Gugger House (later the Merry-Eye Gallery and now the Bicycle Shop). Reports are that Mrs. Gugger "ran it." They report that if the mail arrived before she expected it, she'd rush out, adjusting her corset under a big cloak.

At that time, the mail was brought to Helotes in a two-wheel buggy from "somewhere," Leon Valley? The Shavano railroad whistle-stop off Fredericksburg Road? Evidently later reporters didn't care which.

The postal carrier was black, known simply as N---- - Brody. He'd arrive pulled by a horse wearing a straw hat with holes cut to accommodate the ears. He was under government contract, so nobody had to exchange money. But he was given food and drink, and water for the horse.

People had to drive there (or ride) with saddlebags or gunny sacks (towsacks). Mail for a family and neighbors went into the bag for distribution at the end point.

Here is a sample of the system (with the Marnock Post Office) by several members of the Frank Woller family:

> A Woller, sometimes a teenage girl, rode from the Woller House to the Dolores Cadena House. They saw him/her off to the "other Cadena" House up on that low hill. And they watched until the horse crested the hill down to the Marnock House.
>
> The mail was loaded into two saddlebags. The trip was then reversed. The "other" Cadenas took out their mail. The Dolores Cadenas took out theirs.
>
> Then the Big Event. The Benkes, the Joe (Barefoot) Wollers, Severo Nanez and the Ernst Hausmans gathered to get and share the news that came in the mail—everybody knew everybody else's kinfolks. For instance, Steve Woller's daughter ran off to Schulenberg to become a nun—that was not just family news.
>
> Neighbors met, swapped stories, spread news, shared family events. It was a mini town meeting.

All of that changed (with FDR?) when the Post Office started RFD (Rural Free Delivery) on named or numbered routes, with mailbox locations and numbers. Home or near-home delivery was unthinkable. Large collections of mailboxes were located at major crossroads, sometimes farther than the Helotes Post Office.

But Helotes still had its own. Mrs. Barham was helpful. She could even handle small packages, such as those containing cookies or books or dress patterns or Sears Catalogs.

THE MERRY-EYE

Part 1

Marie Conley, a flower child half-a-century before the others, came to Helotes from San Antonio. "Mrs. Conley" had been living in an apartment in the Irish Flats, a little conclave of artists and musicians near the downtown Post Office. The Irish Flats were razed before necessary (for the City Fathers, any excuse would do), to prepare for decades-away urban renewal.

She bought the Gugger House, and painted the upstairs apartment and its stairwell black to force her tenants to enliven it in their own way.

She and a friend, a short-term partner, opened an art gallery on the bottom floor, with antiques, not many but good. And nobody now can report on the art. The gallery, never advertised except by a sign in the window, was not a success. Helotes wasn't ready for Art, capital A.

Marie was a concert pianist. She introduced Shostakovich and Khachaturian during Max Reiter's tenure with the San Antonio Symphony.

By invitation I saw/heard her as pit pianist for "Parisian Follies" at the Majestic downtown. The music was fluff, but it was a good paycheck for her. I waited for a French composer solo. But no. And anyway, that show introduced Anna Russell to San Antonio. And a "naked" statue under dim blue lighting. A local preacher provided wonderful advertising by objecting to the nudity.

Innocent and even naïve in her ways, she had a bright, quirky mind. Catholic, she walked to Mass down Riggs Road on Sundays. One Sunday she arrived with a nanny goat on a leash—someone had offered it as a gift and she couldn't in her heart refuse it. She explained that the donor did not understand that downtown Helotes was not grazing land. She tied it to a young tree a few paces from the front door. After Mass she asked me if I knew Joe Salek, the director of the San Antonio Little Theatre. Then she asked me to call him and ask whether he wanted to rent her healthy goat—free!—for a play; *Fiddler on the Roof* would need a goat. *Oklahoma,* too.

The next week I reported No to the offer. She said, "But, dear, the Little Theatre could use some realism."

People who were there still remember her July 4, 1976, recital at Guadalupe Church. Helotes had never heard anything like it. Hymns at church, string bands at dance halls, but an organ recital? Never before. Or since.

She took odd piano jobs as orchestra pianist in San Antonio. *They* hadn't forgotten her.

Then Marie became frail. She wore sweaters round the calendar. She wore with panache the only ten-foot scarf anyone had ever seen. And she accepted rides to and from Mass.

Part II

Gradually Marie became ill, unable to manage. She was moved (by whom, we don't know) to a nursing home on Main Street in Boerne. There is little doubt that led to the final decision.

The Guadalupe Church women volunteered to get her home straightened up. Selling it was looming; or giving up on the mortgage. But Mrs. Leo Schott, Mrs. Howard Schott, and Mrs. Red Haby started to find money, big bills, all over the place. As bookmarks, on a shelf in a jar in the kitchen, in random other places, envelopes. Lots of bills. The ladies looked for them, and put them in a brown paper bag. They estimated that they had found about $5,000.

Marie had been cashing her checks (a widow's pension, some early investments, Social Security, performance payments) and putting the cash "at hand."

None of the ladies wanted responsibility for keeping the cash and a few checks overnight. Bad mistake.

They agreed to take it to Father (name withheld), who took it.

They didn't ask for a receipt. Another bad mistake.

Later, questioned by their husbands, Father X dismissed the whole thing as "women's imagination." The bag, as he "remembered" it, had only a few small bills. Trusting their wives, the men demanded honesty. He was adamant.

The next Sunday at the 6:30 Mass, at the Prayers of the faithful (congregational impromptu), John Nanez out loud prayed that God would send Guadalupe a priest who was not a liar and a thief, a disgrace to the parish and the priesthood. Mrs. Nanez reported that Father X stood there dumbstruck with the Nanezes and the other "conspirers," and left the sanctuary without comment.

Then, pandemonium. One woman screamed, "Blasphemy!" Another cried. The men looked at one another communicating: We'll talk to Leo or Howard or Red.

After Mass a group of men followed Father X into the Rectory. They demanded the money or an accounting. He wavered. "If I return it, any of it, I'll be admitting I took it."

Leo suggested that if he returned it, they could say he had been waiting to return it. He declined the offer.

The storm gathered. The men, a larger number by then, called on the D.A. to file felony-theft charges.

Being cautious, the D.A. called the Archbishop while they waited. The Archbishop was direct. "For God's sake the Church has trouble enough without this. Don't rock the boat!" The D.A., citing lack of credible witnesses, hearsay evidence, and lack of apparent motive, declined to accept their charge. The husbands were outraged at the dismissal of their wives as not credible witnesses. The wives' friends in the Altar Society backed them, as did the men of the Holy Name Society. But Father X had his loyal-to-the-death followers, who accused the accusers of ruining his reputation. Libel, they claimed.

A lawyer reminded Father X's supporters that in a libel case, truth is indisputable defense and wins. And all it would take was a print-out of Father X's checking and savings accounts. Continued grumbling replaced conversations.

Then not long afterward word came from the Chancery, via the Marian order, that Father X was being transferred to California for "continued study in ethics" and other subjects. Deadpan irony? Admission?

The money was never recovered.

Marie, well cared for, died in the nursing home in Boerne.

John Nanez left Guadalupe to go to Bulverde.

When St. John Claret opened, there was a sudden influx of parishioners who had been at Guadalupe, some from its beginning. Inexplicably, Father X still comes back now and then for a visit. His adherents celebrate his return.

Nobody ever knew what became of the goat.

THE BARN GHOST

The "other Cadenas" (no kin to Dolores and Soledad, who married the only two boys in that family) lived in the two-story house on the hill off Loop 1604 and Kyle Seele Parkway. It was also home sometime to the Beales, Bob Hayes the water well driller, and others since then. It was the Cadena House at the heart of the legends. *Legends*—plural.

One day some kids from the area—possibly some Benkes, some Wollers (my best source), and certainly some Cadenas—went to the barn to play.

While they were involved with their games, they became aware of a presence, a tall thin black figure. It could be seen through heavy smoke (one said). It was hooded. At least, none of them could see the face. They all agreed that it waved its arms up and down slowly, like a huge bird (a vulture?), flexing its wings. The thing had wide sleeves.

Numbed, silent they stared. Then it "sort of drifted" away from the door. A brave (foolhardy) boy, probably David Cadena, crossed himself and ran to the doorway to see where it had gone. It was gone, probably around the corner of the barn and down the lane leading to the big cattle tank.

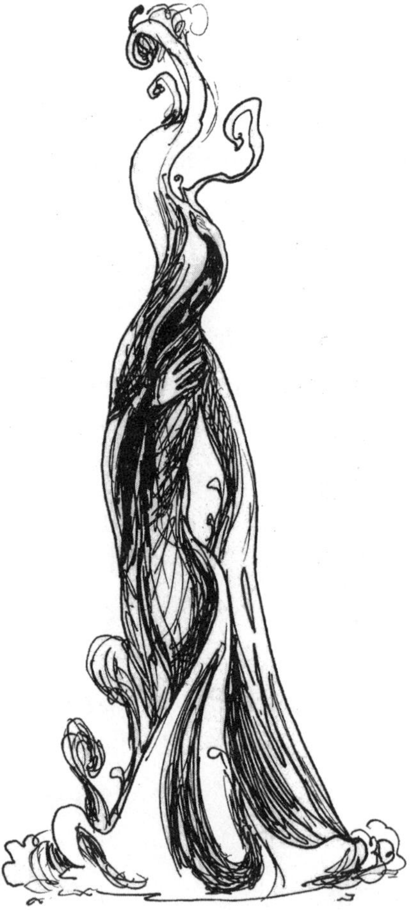

The kids were vocal. They told everybody over and over about seeing a ghost like a shadow. Most of the adults dismissed it as childish imagination. Threatening them with Confession didn't change their story. They saw the thing. That was that.

Carrying his pitchfork (for rattlesnakes, critters), Mr. Cadena walked down the lane. He saw the black figure standing and waiting in the lane. He reported that he confronted it, saying, "From God or from the Devil, you don't scare me. What do you want?"

Immediately the black thing became taller and thinner until it was like a thick column of black smoke. Then it sank into the ground. Mr. Cadena marked the spot and went about his business.

Nobody ever knew what happened next, except that not long afterwards, the Cadenas moved away, into town, bought a house and a car, and David went to the Seminary.

Ghosts and ghost stories bring the curious. After a while, curiosity seekers entered the abandoned house and found the hearthstone pulled up and dropped upside down on the floor. There was a cavity beneath the place where it had been.

The house stood vacant for a long time.

Forty-five or fifty years later, while the house was vacant again, I went to snoop around. I couldn't get in. The thing I remember best is the dog-run between the house and the detached kitchen.

LUCY'S TREASURES

Lucy Perkins Brown had a journalist's yen for glamorous copy. And a schoolgirl's lack of critical thinking. She also had an inventive, fertile imagination, tending to fantasy.

When she and her publisher-husband, Charles, moved the *Helotes Echo* to the storied Marnock "Mansion" (her label), they came into possession of the frequently plowed and tilled little field (double-lawn size) between the house and road. Sometime back it had been the Marnock kitchen garden.

Somehow one day, presumably preparing to plant something, she and Charles and maybe a worker, hit a long stone, about three feet long and six inches in diameter. It did not seem like the field stones from thereabouts or like creek stones—the Helotes Creek was just across the road.

Aha! It is a petrified mastodon tusk. She remembered reading that millions of years ago, before all of this part of Texas was underwater, mastodons "probably" lived here. And she had the proof.

There were admirers and doubters. One said it looked like a broken-off stalactite.

She said she was going to have the tusk authenticated "by a university." Oddly, nobody ever read or heard of the results.

Some scoffers wondered where the rest of that huge skeleton went. No problem: It washed away when the ocean receded.

Nobody has reported whatever became of the object. It is too big to be misplaced.

But Lucy was undeterred, and a slow learner.

Same little field; same human cast. An object in the well-plowed field looked like carved stone or molded and fired ceramic. It struck her as vaguely familiar.

Aha! It was the broken-off head of a Mayan statue. Eye of the beholder.

There were practical logistic problems: How did the broken statue head get from Yucatan to Central Mexico and then across a major desert and northeast across the Rio Grande into Central Texas and then to a family garden on Scenic Loop Road at the foot of the hill country? She dismissed that: "They brought it with them." She remembered that the Mayans were famous explorers.

A few people gaped at the art treasure. She circulated photos of the Mayan Prince.

Then with the sale of the Marnock House to its current owners and the sale of the *Echo*, details blurred.

Where are the artifacts? Lucy and Charley have died.

Asking around has not produced an answer.

MURDER I

From most reports, Maxey Benke was a wannabe. He wanted to run with the Big Guys. He wore better clothes than his siblings, with spats, and he bought a Touring Car—all with no visible means of support.

Rumor and gossip said he was "mixed up" with moonshiners and bootleggers. He did favors for his new friends and they rewarded him—for contacts and deliveries? He was an errand runner. It was the good life.

Then one Sunday morning, on call, the Sheriff found Maxey's body in his car just beyond the wooden bridge on Mockingbird Lane just off Fredericksburg Road, about a mile townward from Eight Mile Hill.

He was shot to death sitting at the steering wheel.

The Sheriff declared that there were no clues, no suspects, no apparent motive. Maybe an enraged husband? But it was probably a liquor deal gone bad. Anyway, the case was closed.

But it didn't die right there. Alice Igo Bowman and her husband Henry reported that on their way home from a dance at Braun Hall, they passed Benke's gate and saw Maxey's car, parked just inside the property, off the road going up the hill to the European-style Benke compound.

But there's a problem with that, too. The Benke gate was a destination at the end of a dirt lane off Hausman Road. If they saw Maxey's car, they were snooping, not driving past. But it could help fix the time of the murder—after the dance but before dawn.

That problematic evidence made no difference, although she told it to the end of her life. In her dimming she thought she remembered seeing his body.

The case was closed and remains closed.

THE WHITE WITCH

She had a strong, clear voice her listeners called sweet. She was invited to sing at weddings and funerals. She sang on request, but never at church. That detail was noted later.

She was a good hostess when members of her family or extended family came for an afternoon visit, many afoot. She introduced switchel to the community—a beverage of brown sugar, vinegar, and water, a kind of substitute root beer.

But she was distrusted. Everybody "knew" she was a sharp dealer, taking an advantage in a deal.

One Sunday after Mass she and her son drove northward from Prue Road, past the snake place and alongside the pear orchard, and found trespassers a half-mile inside her NO TRESPASSING sign. They were picnicking, with a fire going, rimmed with new copper cookware. With a double-barreled shotgun at the ready, she invited them to leave and confiscated. Years later she gave the largest pot to my mother to use at butchering time—it was just the right size for rendering cracklings.

She cheated on handshake deals and advised "Get it in writing."

The community was agape when she committed perjury in court (unchallenged and unpunished) in order to get possession of seventy-seven acres of hay meadow her late husband had co-owned with two brothers. She claimed she needed the productive land to provide for her little son (who was about sixteen at the time). Pity the poor crying widow won the day.

She also claimed kin to Robert E. Lee and saw to it that one of her nephews was given that name.

She generated a troubled atmosphere. The air was pregnant. Then it came.

An ordinarily level-headed German dairy farmer, over there across a field and a road, accused her of stealing milk from cows, one of which, a good producer, suddenly gave almost no milk. It looked as if the cow had been milked dry.

She was a White Witch.

That charge is hard to refute and even harder to forget. In time it might have died from inattention and intervening scandal elsewhere. But her two youngest nieces, bored during a switchel visit, went nosing around in the milk barn. There they found a board about eighteen inches long, four wide, with four one-inch holes augured into it, several inches apart. In each hole there was a four- or five-inch piece of one-inch rope. Farm girls, they had never seen anything like it.

Aha! The witch's cowbag.

They kept their discovery to themselves till supper, when they told the whole family. Papa said No; Mama said Maybe. The oldest son (who told me) said he had heard of other cases like it. That was it.

Nobody ever found the magic device, and nobody could figure out the "real" use of the object. There is no mention again of the German's robbed cow.

Some of the Settlement men said she was tough enough to sing at her own funeral.

After years of being visited only by her family, including Robert E. Lee, she died, as they say, full of years.

MURDER II

Two locally prominent brothers lived close to each other in the area southwest of Loop 1604 and Highway 16 (Bandera Road).

One day somebody called about hearing gunshots, a rifle. The Sheriff's deputy found one of the wives dead, shot from behind (in the head?) sitting at the table on a kitchen chair.

The deputy found a man's footprints from her door to the other house, to and from. The Sheriff arrived and ruled that here was no solid evidence, only circumstantial. He noted that there was no suspect, no clues, no known motive.

Case closed, leaving neighbors puzzled and angered. They knew *who*.

ARTIFACTS

Ross Barham ran a business just outside downtown Helotes, before Scenic Loop Road. He sold cedar posts and associated items.

But his hobby was the American Indian. He had found middens on low bluffs overlooking the Helotes Creek. He found several "fine" pieces, which he sent to the University of Texas for their collection. He had thank-you letters from a curator there. He felt he had become part of history.

But he had heard of Painted Rock, Texas, and other places where Indians left marks (messages?). He wanted to find something—anything—to indicate these "local" Indians could do that.

One Saturday afternoon Ross and his wife (who was post-mistress when she told the story) tramped up and down the Helotes Creek bed, from the Blue Hole to Marnock's. She usually went along on Saturdays, her time off, "to indulge him."

He scouted ahead. She called out to him to ask if "this" was the kind of thing he meant. It was a "mano" or "celt" with four or five parallel lines over an inch long, scratched deeply into its surface. That could not have been an accident.

Elated, he wrote to the curator at UT.

So now, the only known example of a hand-worked artifact from the Helotes area is in Austin, courtesy of Ross Barham, of Helotes, Texas.

Mrs. Barham said, “When I remind him that MY name should be on it, he gets grumpy.”

CLETO

Cleto lived in a stone house, on a hill that sloped sharply down to the Leon Creek. It was one big room with a massive fireplace and one door he could barricade.

Cleto was a scaredy-cat. Alarm was his way of living. He lived in agitated fear of robbers, rattlesnakes, Indians (*especially* Indians), thunderstorms, gangsters and outlaws, mountain lions, hail, and tainted meat. There were perch in pools in the Leon, but they were beneath consideration. He lived mostly on beans and the squirrels and rabbits his in-laws brought him.

His brother-in-law, to snap him out of it, organized a group of men to meet with him to teach Cleto a practical lesson, for his own good. They waited until his coal-oil lamp went out, then they went wild, screaming, making "Indian" noises. One fired a pistol.

They waited a while. Then they broke in the door to show him it was all right, that it was just friends and neighbors.

No Cleto.

He could not have escaped—he was not under the bed or behind the blanket box by the woodstove.

One of them spotted his feet in the chimney. They tried to pull him down. He was kicking and screaming, cussing and praying.

They got him down after a struggle. One lit his lamp so he could see them. They dusted soot off him. Someone gave him a drink from the dipper hanging in the crock.

Calmed finally, he asked if they had seen those savage Indians in the war-party, waiting to kill him.

"There were no Indians."

"Yes there were! For hours they circled this house with horses. And then my friends came and scared the Indians away with a gunshot. "

Cleto said he'd be grateful till his dying day, with a sign of the Cross at that point. And he was. What had been a sheltered shy man became a public teller of the tale of his rescue from savages by Christians.

They gave up.

The next year he moved.

MR. BRAUCHLE'S SCHOOL

Mr. Brauchle's school sat back off Bandera Road, not far from Helotes Creek. He created the school because a school was necessary, to accommodate families from the Settlement area. Children walked or rode ponies from long distances. My mother's oldest siblings went there.

Mrs. Brauchle, unacknowledged, was a teacher's helper, but she did half the work.

Pupils learned Reading, Writing, Ciphering, and Estimating in the morning. Some American History, some Classic legends. No recess.

After lunch, brown bag or tin bucket, the boys went with Mr. Brauchle, and the girls gathered with Mrs. Brauchle.

The boys learned, hands-on, the elements of farming: how to make or mend a bridle, how to use a one-horse plow, when to plant (Washington's Birthday was a Settlement favorite for corn), how to place watermelons and cantaloupes (muskmelons) in cornrows, how to doctor minor ailments of animals, how to milk a cow. The boys actually planted and tended Mr. Brauchle's own crops.

The girls learned housekeeping/homemaking: how to make soap and candles, how to sew and embroider aprons. How to prepare and cook meats and seasonal vegetables, how to separate cream, then churn and mold butter, how to sew without patterns and how to darn socks, how to trim a good dress with lace, how to make cottage cheese, simple preserving techniques, how to prepare and bake fancy or plain bread, how to chop kindling for woodstoves, how to iron with stove-heated flatirons. They learned about spices and herbs.

The student body was mostly stable, except for seasonal planting or harvesting.

The price? Who knows? Nobody later ever mentioned it. Barter, maybe?

Those kids grew up to be munitions handlers, a grounds engineer for Swift, a telephone operator, an Air Force wife, a bookkeeper, a fireman, a monument carver. All of them praised the Brauchle School. One said: "The mornings were easy. Those afternoons were hard work!" That one became a ranch foreman.

SCARING INDIANS

After the Civil War there were still "Indian raids," mostly nocturnal horse thievery. They were cautious; they wrapped their hooves in gunny sacks for silence.

Children, especially girls, were given instructions. But boys, too, were cautioned to hide: Indians stole boys to replace their dead warriors. "White Indians."

One day the people in Soledad Cadena's house were gone—into Helotes or Leon Valley? Somewhere.

They left behind (with severe warnings) a girl of about ten (who grew up to become the mother of Louis "Looey" Rodriguez, the tombstone merchant).

She heard horses, several. Indians coming up the hill in broad daylight. She went into action with a mercurochrome bottle. She gave herself red spots with the glass rod. Then she jumped into bed and pulled up the covers.

The Indian walked around downstairs and came up the stairs. When he came into the room she cowered away from him.

He came to the bed and pulled back the sheet. He saw the spots. He let out a scream (which she imitated later). He fled, yelling to the other Indians. They raced away.

In both Cadena sisters' houses she became a heroine.

THE KID

Frank Nikolaus Woller, the elder, somehow met the right person at the right time while he was on a trip into San Antonio for supplies. He thought later that it had been in the little park across the street from the Market House where employers hired short-term workers. A handshake was a "man's bond."

He became "the Kid" (age sixteen, if that) on what turned out to be the last cattle drive out of Bexar (he pronounced it bex-ĕr) County to the railheads in Kansas.

He was gone about two years. He didn't talk about it much—maybe an occasional incident.

He left a youth. He came back a man, with a mustache (his large oval sepia portrait stayed in his family). He and his brothers, Joe and Alois, built him a house of caliche blocks, which is still standing on Woller Road. He married, all of that, before the birth of his first child in 1888, a daughter named Cecilia for his otherwise unidentified "first girlfriend."

He returned with skills useful on the farm, splicing bridles and the like. But the one he entertained the family with he could do into middle age. He could take a broomstick, a hand at each end, and jump over it. His sons couldn't.

There is no record of his being in that cattle drive. The docent at the Trail Drivers Museum was not surprised. Record keeping cowboys?

SAM'S INNOCENT HEART

When Sam Benke was not taking care of farm busy work he stood by his Hausman Road gate, watching everything—what little he could see of his neighbors and traffic.

So it was that one day he watched as an unmarked white van backed into Colley's driveway. In a little while two men in unlabeled coveralls came out, carrying Colley's TV.

Sam went over and asked them about their work. TV repair, overnight. That was impressive. Since his "machine" was "jumping," he asked them to come over and take his along.

They agreed, readily.

Sam held the door for them, unplugged his machine, and closed the gate behind them.

That night, those who knew of Sam's vigilance came over to ask if he had seen a truck. Yes, white van, company unmarked. "Well, they stole my TV."

Sam rubbed his jaw as usual when he was trying to think about something new. But he didn't tell Colley the rest of the story.

His children, Verna Belle and Raymond, told it later at school, as a friendly warning.

JULY 4, 1976

[This story first appeared in *First Timers and Old Timers: The Texas Folklore Society Fire Burns On*, PTFS #68, 2012—*Untiedt*]

Instead of a sermon that day, Our Lady of Guadalupe Church in Helotes had an organ recital by Marie Conley. Without preamble, Father Louis Trawalter introduced her.

She was old, *old*—upper '80s, maybe '90s—but her fingers were agile. I can believe that she had introduced Khachaturian, Shostakovich, and Prokofiev to San Antonio with Max Reiter decades back, from her house/studio in the now long-gone Irish Flats. Her program was unannounced and there were no printed programs: "The National Emblem March," a Stephen Foster, a colonial tune, "Battle Hymn of the Republic," "Tenting on the Old Camp Ground," an unfamiliar 19th century hymn, a minstrel show tune, "Rock of Ages," a spiritual, a George M. Cohan song, "America the Beautiful," "I Love You Truly," and "Dixie." Every resource of that organ was called into use: whispering, humming, fluting, booming, with bugle effects, drum effects, crashing and roaring, and chiming. Her "Battle Hymn of the Republic" was enough to give hackles; it was a *martial* hymn, with drums and muskets in it. It was not a pious sentimentality but a triumphant war cry. Her Hallelujahs floated over drums.

Then she started into "Dixie." Marie Conley was old enough that her parents would have had personal experience of the Civil War—and it remained with her, probably from childhood family stories. Her "Dixie" started somewhere off there in a mist, almost like music drifting across water, as if memory-blurred. Then she saw it more clearly, and the vision sharpened and the notes came clearer. The distance faded.

Old emotions became new again; forgotten responses stirred and awoke. And those old fingers willed an urgency, a commitment, and an exultation that performances over the years have forgotten. The organ swelled and opened. A cause long-lost now, a way of life that has been prettified into romance, a cultural identity obscured by time and clichés came through—direct, strong, beautiful, and doomed. That organ spoke as it never had before, and never would again. Marie Conley, in a tacky old-fashioned blue dress and white blouse, with a ten-foot red Isadora Duncan scarf, leaning over the keys to be sure of her skills, became the Pied Piper, a Sibyl, and Bard recounting the history of the tribe. "Dixie" crashed to a halt and hung there, not to be violated. The pause after she finished was an exquisite tribute.

Then the applause started and swelled, and went on and on—and on. She had reached more deeply into her listeners than they had realized. One young woman with a small child was crying openly.

After Mass, I spoke with Marie briefly. She was elated at the response. Then she said, "Dear, it wasn't right—it wasn't just *right*!"

"It was perfect," I replied.

"No, dear. I wanted to do a little 'Rhapsody in Blue'—it should be there—but I couldn't work it in."

"Your 'Battle Hymn' and 'Dixie' couldn't need help. You did everything but a cowboy song."

She looked at me. "That 19th century hymn wasn't a hymn—it was an … arrangement." She smiled a conspiratorial smile and said, to head off comment, "Would you see me to the car, now, dear?" Holding my arm, that fragile little old lady left the church door, regally, through a group of awed neighbors. Elizabeth Schwarzkopf, that most regal of all singers, would have stumbled with envy at the sight.

After she was gone, Father Trawalter said, "I didn't know what I was turning loose."

I said, "You should hear her 'Can-Can'!"

"You knew didn't you? But the 'Can-Can'—I'm glad she didn't work it in."

"Are you sure she didn't?" He looked at me. I went on, "She has a gift for… arrangements."

He just smiled.

THE FENCE

One of the residents along the Scenic Loop Road decided to re-fence his property. Spools of barbed wire and tools were deposited alongside the old fence.

An enterprising young man decided that they must have been abandoned and put them into his two-wheeler.

As he was finishing, Mr. Menchaca came by, toward Helotes in his light wagon. He lectured the young man sternly, calling it theft and vandalism, sinful and felonious. The young man gave up and helped Mr. Menchaca load the fence wire and tools onto his wagon. The young man left quickly.

On toward town, Mr. Menchaca met Dr. Marnock in his two-wheeler, on a medical mission. Dr. Marnock asked about the obviously new wire. Mr. Menchaca told the story. Dr. Marnock found it convenient to ask Mr. Menchaca to help him transfer the wire to the back of the doctor's buggy.

They loaded the wire and Dr. Marnock went his way, telling Mr. Menchaca that he would keep the wire until someone came to claim it. Since he didn't need them, he left the tools with Mr. Menchaca "for his service."

Who knew to ask? After several months, nobody claimed it.

So Dr. Marnock declared it abandoned and used it to fence his plowed and fenced little field in front of his house.

THE FAMOUS STEW

Frank Woller the younger's dog, Blue, came down with something. Blue was very old, but that was overlooked. Members of the family pampered him with cottontails and squirrels, some raw, some cooked.

Young Frank killed a large wood rat in the barn he and Celestino Sanchez used as a bunkhouse. He left it on the kitchen table, intending to chop it up for Blue that evening.

When young Frank came in for lunch from the field, Grandma was gone somewhere nearby—you could tell by the state of the fire in the woodstove.

He found his lunch, a stew on the back of the stove. He helped himself, adding salt, pepper, and a dash of chili pitin sauce.

That evening, when Frank senior, son George, and the family mozo, Celestino, came in, they had fried sausage, potatoes, and flour tortillas.

Young Frank asked about the cottontail stew.

What cottontail? Oh. The wood rat for Blue!

OUR LADY OF ZION

For decades Helotes had only two churches, Zion Lutheran and Los Reyes, followed by Guadalupe. Had to choose. Residents intermarried. A practice, officially disapproved, was that girls went to mother's church, and boys went to father's church. Mixed marriages, mixed families, mixed congregations.

The relationship between the churches was familial, also. Once, the Lutherans donated the terrazzo tile for the sanctuary of the Catholic Church. When either church had a bazaar or other festivity (barbecues), the crowd was a mixture.

When the Lutheran ladies helped the Catholic ladies with a parish Mexican supper, they brought sauerkraut.

When either group was raising money for a major project, they knocked on doors of either/both without asking or mentioning affiliations. And people gave to either/both. They were neighbors and sometimes relatives, not congregations.

So it was that the Lutheran pastor was out gathering donations toward starting the new church on Leslie Road. He knocked on all doors.

He knocked on the Rectory door at Guadalupe and explained that he was not asking for a donation. He simply wanted Father Rabe to know he was knocking on all doors.

Father Rabe reported the next Sunday that he asked the pastor to wait a minute. He went into his office and came out with a $1500 check. The pastor asked if that was allowed—giving aid and comfort to "an heretical sect" was probably forbidden by Canon Law.

Father Rabe waved that aside and explained he'd probably gain divine credit. His congregation was not giving to help build the new church on Leslie Road—the Guadalupe people were donating the money to help tear down the old one.

WATERMELONS

For a century more or less the Benkes (Hungarian) and their daughter's family (Alsatian) lived side-by-side with the Wollers (Bavarian). From all reports across a generation or two it was amicable with a few minor problems. Kids!

One day, Annie and Henry Woller went through their own watermelon patch, crossed the fence into Benke's, and took an attractive large watermelon.

On the way home they found Maxey Benke in the Woller field, carrying a large, attractive watermelon.

It was the joke of the season on both sides of the fence.

INFANT MORTALITY

Infant mortality ran high. My maternal grandparents lost two girls in infancy; ten children survived.

Children, everyone believed, were the only guaranteed immortality. If a couple died childless or if the children preceded the parents, it was a sort of community grief—the end of the line.

Severo Nanez outdid the immortality idea. But he added a twist that turned to legend. He named every one of the boys Severo, with various middle names.

School records went haywire.

His second wife had more sons, so that he had seven in all—no girls.

I knew the oldest. Severo John, who was easily five years my senior. My sister, a decade behind me, was in classes with a younger one, Severo Something.

He won. He left not only his line, but his *name.*

THE NAME: A PLACE WITH THREE MOTHERS

By far the most popular idea about the name, *Helotes*, derives from a bit of charming folklore, championed as valid by a local historian.

This one is based on an anecdote in which a cartographer, meeting a native carrying a sack, asks the name of the place. The Spanish-only native, not understanding, answered, "Elotes" (roasting ears) for the contents of the sack.

That creates a problem. Why would a cartographer add a breathed "H" before the word?

Another theory of origin was just seriocomic, too kooky for serious consideration until Alex Parrigin, a local realtor, had a gobbler share the top of the front page of his monthly newspaper, *The Helotes Herald*—two crossed ears of corn with a gobbler. People nodded and grinned, remembering having heard that version years before.

Briefly, in the 1940s–'50s, when John Floore took over the Riggs store, once monthly he produced/published a giveaway newsletter/newspaper called "The Z Room," which mentioned corn and turkeys. He moved his business diagonally across the road to its current location. "The Z Room" died.

The turkey theory has the cartographer, native, sack, and question. But the answer was "Guajalotes" (turkeys plural), which the cartographer understood as, Why, Helotes!"

The third one is less colorful but not necessarily valid, either. For decades traveling dealers set up their wagons-with-wares on a regular schedule each month, making a mobile mall. They gathered on the "town" side of Helotes Creek on the flat by Elf Industries (now).

The peddlers were Greek, Syrian, Ayrab (remember the peddler in *Oklahoma*?). They were considered as untrustworthy as Gypsies were, later. Someone (a Greek peddler?) called them the Greek equivalent of inferior/low class/menial, "Helotes." *Helot* in the singular. So: The Place of the Lowdown Greek Peddlers?

Wanda Terry (right name?), the mother of the owners of the Hickory Hut, told me the name of the first peddler to set up there was Manczak (man-shack), a folkloric origin of the later resident family of Menchaca—of Polish origin, folks said.

Even so, nobody *knows* how Helotes got its name.

The best treatment of the topic is to be found in the writings of Cynthia Leal Massey. But she is not dealing in folklore.

LILY'S BOTTLE

Mrs. Riggs of Riggs Store had an employee, Lily, who was indispensable. Lily could do it. Lily did it: selling, restocking, maintenance, janitorial work, cashiering, P-R, anything, everything.

Mrs. Riggs kept a big bottle (was it really a Coke bottle?) on the counter behind the cashier. Every day she dropped one dime into the bottle.

For Christmas, she emptied the bottle and gave the $36.50 to Lily as a bonus. Back then, $36 was a hefty sum.

ST. CECILIA'S EYES

On a dark, clear night, people would try to find/see St. Cecilia's Eyes. They were a pair of stars in the Southeastern sky, about 45° up. Seeing them was good, comforting, a kind of blessing.

As a child I used to look to find them. Frequently I saw them.

Skip forty years.

A teaching friend living in Grey Forest, but teaching in Schertz-Cibolo, called me one morning early to tell me that the evening before he had seen St. Cecilia's Eyes. The practice came racing back. Folk belief, yes, but influential.

My grandfather, Frank Woller, named his first child Cecilia. She died in infancy. He gave the name Cecilia to his daughter, Gertrude. He wanted their benign influence in his family.

A superstition maybe? But it was passed along as folklore. A public school teacher from Cuero-San Antonio-Austin-Grey Forest knew about St. Cecilia's Eyes, without local prompting.

2.
4.
6.
5.
3.
7.
1.
9.
8.
11.
12.

THE WALTZ CONTEST

The Helotes Dance Hall held Waltz Contests now and then, open to any couple. There were prizes. The Dance Hall had what we would now call a country band, with no singing. The dances usually ended about eleven with "Goodnight, Sweetheart," but when they ran late (midnight or even one), the band played "It's Three O'clock in the Morning."

The Waltz Contest rules were strict, refereed by four males, one on each side of the dance floor. Any infraction brought "Out 1!" The couples' heels could not touch the floor; they had to dance around the floor, past each referee.

A lifetime later, I remember one contest vividly. My father and mother won, again. I was not with Mr. Biering that night. They wanted me to be there because they expected to win, again.

After the winners were announced, the custom was to have the winners do an exhibition solo with the other couples standing around the floor. My father came to get me where I sat watching beside one of the Braendle girls. He took me onto the floor. They cradled me, their hands on each other's shoulders. I remember the joy of being whirled around the floor. They said I didn't go to sleep on the way home, as I usually did.

STORY-TELLER

Mr. Biering was a large man. I never saw him standing. He was always sitting in a kind of white wicker wing-back chair, dressed in a white linen suit.

In those days there were no babysitters. The choices: take them along, leave them with relatives, or stay home. Some of the take-alongs were given a slug of paregoric and slept through the whole event in the car.

No one now knows how it developed, but Mr. Biering became a babysitter for several kids at a time. He "sat" only when there were dances at Riggs' Helotes Dance Hall. There must have been some sort of monetary arrangement, but I was far too young to notice.

A parent would come in and drop off the kid(s). I do not remember that any of the kids cried. All that time Mr. Biering was already talking.

The kids sat in irregular semicircles on the carpet. He told stories continuously, mostly amusing, but some cautionary. If a kid got sleepy, he/she simply toppled to one side and slept. When the parent(s) returned Mr. Biering was still talking. I do not remember that there were words exchanged among them. The kid was picked up, literally, sometimes still asleep.

My childhood was enhanced by those stories. I remember one in particular. Many of his stories were autobiographical. Of course, over several visits I heard some stories several times. I had a favorite. As a boy Mr. Biering used to walk to school, across Bandera Road to Mr. Brauchle's school, a quarter of a mile through the sparse (mesquite) woods. He noticed a cottontail every morning. He hunched to convey the little rabbit. It sat beside the trail looking the other way. (He demonstrated.) It wouldn't run until he was almost upon it. Winter came. (He shivered.) He thought the bunny must be cold. (He did a bunny-shiver.) He planned to catch it and take it home to protect it. (He nodded approval.)

One cold winter day, he acted. He tiptoed to the rabbit from the downwind side. It sat there shivering. He got close enough to grab it. He grabbed it.

He said it took four grown men two hours to "help" him turn that thing loose.

Then he laughed a big sharing laugh. And all the kids laughed, too.

STRINGTOWN: AN ELEGY

Villages usually cluster around a church, a big employing business, a country store, or crossroads. A hamlet is smaller than a village.

In the 1920s and '30s and even into the '40s, Stringtown was a hamlet with a difference. It had no center as a cluster would. It was linear, strung out, hence Stringtown. It occupied Babcock Road from the De Zavala junction to Prue Road, from the Stutts (or Stutz) home southward to the Braendle house on the south, on Prue Road, where the gravel road ended.

There were only two houses on the east side, but nine on the west. Four of them were rented out from time to time. Renters were seldom transitory. Most residents knew them. *They* became residents.

Of course, everybody knew everybody and all their business: kinfolks, ailments, employment, temperament, religion, education, and family origins. The residents were, more or less, like-minded about basics. At least they could state a consensus with accuracy. A census (1932–33) brought interviewers, who could get solid information, if someone was gone for the day, to be easily and quickly verified later.

And there were kinfolks. Rosetta Montgomery was kin to Piercy Benke; Mina Woller was the sister of Mrs. Hoffman. Along the way, when the Whetstones moved away they were replaced by Anton Woller who was brother-in-law to Mina Woller. Mrs. Hoffman's renter, Henry Bowman, was a brother-in-law of Johnny Igo, who rented the two-story Michaelson-Benke two-story house. And for a while the Ed Igo family lived in Mrs. Hoffman's rent house, until they moved to Rosetta Montgomery's property, which they bought.

Stringtown was like one extended family.

Stringtown had flowers, in front yards in orderly rows or on front porches. The Michaelson-Benke house was noted for its giant tame sunflowers on its north side by the rainwater cistern, and Four-o'clocks on the south.

There were no pianos in Stringtown. Nobody played an instrument, except harmonicas and "Jews' Harps," which could be heard at night coming from bunkhouses where hired help slept. There were, factually, two instruments, ten years apart. In the late 1920s, Eddie Igo decided he wanted a trombone. He bought one from the San Antonio Music Company downtown on Commerce Street. Somehow he had gotten the notion that owning an instrument meant he could play it immediately, without practice. He reported that he sat on his front porch, blowing through. No luck. "I was blowing my brains out. I never got the knack of it." After a week or so, he sold it back to the company and gave up music.

In the late 1930s, his nephew, Harris Bowman, developed a yen for a black and red concertina. His grandmother gave him one for Christmas. All of those buttons spooked him. He couldn't make it work—all that came out was noise. He sold it when he was drafted in World War II.

In Stringtown nobody sang, except while working. Mr. Knudsen sang "Springtime in the Rockies" over and over and over while doing chores. And Annie Igo sang at her sewing machine, sentimental ballads and songs popular in the 1890s. No instruments and no singers, but also there were no phonographs.

Dealers came to Stringtown, as a destination, not by chance. The Watkins man came with salves, vanilla extract, hand balm for milkers, fig cough syrup, dandruff cures, herbal cigarettes for asthmatics, bluing for keeping white linens white, liniment, Bay Rum, red hair oil, tar soap, and 3-in-1 oil for sewing machines. The salesman offered also an array of horse products: hoof-oil, shampoo, and worm remedies. On his own, as a sort of under-the-counter, he offered Paris Green and London Purple, both toxic pesticides. He warned people not to stand downwind while applying the mercury-based powders to ant beds and the like.

Mr. Nichols out of San Antonio brought coal-oil for stoves, heaters, and lamps. If he came midweek he sometimes had a few blocks of ice. Orchard owners or peddlers brought freestone or clingstone peaches from Fredericksburg, in season. They came in converted coupes, with trunk lids removed.

The meat man came once a week, with ice-cooled fresh meat, including illegal venison (ah, venison chili!). His customers never betrayed him, even to Hitzfelder, the Game Warden.

Some of the reasons that Stringtown was fated to die were that there was no church (although there are two now). There was no store really, but Rosetta Montgomery and her family, the Michaelsons, built and ran a tiny convenience store lacking a gasoline pump. They had a few regular customers for Sunday newspapers and store-bought bread (for emergencies), cookies, and a few essentials such as matches. It failed and was razed, leaving only some concrete steps going nowhere.

Most important was the lack of a central meeting place for the exchange of ideas and recipes. There was no spokesman for Stringtown, and no honorary Mayor, as Helotes had. Helotes even named a road for their honorary Mayor.

Of less importance was the lack of a place to "go eat," of the kind in Helotes one way, or over on Fredericksburg Road the other way. Also, there was no place to buy beer, hooch, or wine. Prohibition was stifling. Not that it mattered in Stringtown. People made their own beer, wine (ah, agarita wine!), and a heady peach brandy. Most households had a hygrometer for gauging the ripeness of beer. Most of the men knew a bootlegger anyway.

There was no blacksmith, no names on the gates—mailboxes were somewhere else, down the road northward. All the Stringtown mailboxes, called Route Two, were on Babcock, outside the Stutts's fence, directly across the road from Teddo Benke's Skeleton House. And there was no public telephone, and not many houses had one.

Stringtown was a totally dependent suburb. San Antonio slowly swallowed it. But it was not a bedroom suburb. Stringtowners did not have jobs in the city.

Childhood diseases did not sweep through Stringtown, even though all the children went to Lock Hill School, at that time still a county school. They'd hear of an isolated case of mumps (caught from an adult dairy worker), chickenpox, or "roseola." One five-year-old boy in the Michaelson-Benke house had Rheumatic Fever, and Buster Braendle died of a mastoid infection. Adults and old-timers had aches and pains and an occasional "hitch in their gitalongs." But there were no crutches, except temporary, and no wheelchairs. There are no reports of gout. There was no cancer, no T.B., and no heart disease (that anyone knew of).

Every Stringtowner with cows had a DeLaval hand-cranked cream separator, to provide cream for churning butter and for "drip cheese" (a.k.a. cottage cheese now). But Piercy Benke had a trove of implements to fascinate Yvonne Stutts (Ya-honey) and all the other kids. In a spare room (one room with dividers, really), she had a hand-cranked corn-sheller that kicked out corncobs she used as kindling to start the wash-fires under her three-foot diameter, heavy half-shell where she hand-scrubbed the men's workclothes with homemade lye soap, under her pampered but grapeless grapevine arbor.

She also had two boards (5 × 8 inches) with useful-grip handles and a thousand half-inch spikes on each for carding wool to make thread—she didn't knit, but relatives did.

She also had a no-kill rat-trap for capturing barn rats in the corncrib, no matter that Junior, her retarded son, drowned them in the cattle tank just south of the house. She also had a rod-like contraption, a fence stretcher, a ratchet that tightened a single strand of barbed wire and held it while the wire was being stapled to a cedar post. She ignored the fact that her oldest son, Alley (Alexander) had borrowed it from Johnny Igo and had not returned it. She also had a de-horner and Bluemel's feed-store mercury thermometer.

She was a tough lender. But her "room" contained, in a sense, the working-history of Stringtown.

Every house had a gutter and spout system for collecting rainwater, which was used sparingly for laundry, since rainwater is soft. The Benkes had an underground cistern with a pump; all the others used cisterns (like cattle troughs) or barrels.

There were no orchards, except a small pear orchard across Babcock Road from Teddo Benke's big field, outside Stringtown a hundred feet away. It was regularly raided.

Despite the persuasions and dire warnings of door-to-door peddlers, there were no lightning rods in Stringtown. The idea was, apparently, that the rods attracted lightning, so why pay for that?

About half of the men in Stringtown hunted deer. The space above their garage or barn door proved their successes—much like notches in a pistol grip two generations earlier. One man (name withheld) had over a hundred sets of antlers (shhhh!). Two-a-season legally could not account for that.

Alice Igo Bowman was the only recorded woman deer-hunter. In the pre-slacks era, she wore her son's pants and jacket. She climbed trees and deer-blind towers. And she had one buck-head mounted for display—but never displayed it. She kept it in their garage.

Only the barn-red Stutts house, Mrs. Hoffman's rent house, and Mina Woller's rent house had easily-seen water towers. Mrs. Hoffman's rent house water tower was boxed in and served as a bathhouse. A portable kerosene heater didn't help much in cold weather. She added a bathroom in a previous alcove across the hall from the (warm) kitchen.

After Mina Woller's death, there was an estate sale by auction. Stringtowners by unspoken consent let someone who "really wanted it" place the only (and low) bid. If a neighbor wanted the sauerkraut crock, she got in. The coal-oil lamp with the hand-stained florentined chimney went to another neighbor without competition. But a few outsiders outbid the locals on some items. They were there to invest in artifacts. Locals were there to keep memorabilia. An old quilt went for $300 even though no locals bid on it. A local bid $15 for Mina's father's or grandfather's six-inch long telescoping brass spyglass; an outsider jumped that on the next bid to $35 and took it home with her a local "landmark." And the handpainted Muhl board from Germany, that Mina and the little boy from across the road had used, using red beans and butter-beans as game pieces, went to a stranger. Locals had not expected high bids and had not brought more cash to the cash-only auction.

But Mina's curling-iron that was hinged to hang in the chimney of a kerosene lamp was sold to a pleased local. Mina's son's cattle brand, CW, sold at low bid and after changing hands several times, twice there, it ended (for $35) in the possession of Jodi Kouri, a Woller great-great niece. A prized stereoscope with a basket of stereo cards from Germany, with German texts, mostly buildings, bridges, fountains, aqueducts, classic ruins, memorials—all in deep sepia prints—went to an outsider, a woman who jumped the local standard bid of $15 to $75. A local reported that the disapproval was so evident that she hurried away. As she left, several local men whose wives were disappointed said things to her nobody else could hear. She sped away.

For several years some of the men got together to play cards, probably not poker. It was a comfortable arrangement. Then they decided that they were really a club, with "members." And innocently, believe it or don't, they decided to be a branch of the KKK—the costumes, evidently, were the lure. According to two of them, separately, they didn't know about the real KKK and never contacted the parent organization. They had no agenda, and certainly nothing racist: one of their members was Severo Nanez, Sr., who may have been drawn by the beer.

Lena Gerfers Igo designed and sewed Eddie Igo's gown with a detachable hood. The others obviously managed in their own way. Then they decided to have a parade—

all eight, nine, or ten of them. There had never been a parade in Stringtown—and none since. They spread the word so they could have a crowd watch them show off. They marched (no: strolled) through Stringtown from the south, at Prue Road. They found a few curious, idle neighbors here and there, watching. There were catcalls at the hooded figures: "Eddie, I'd know you anywhere," "Frank (Bluemel), is that you?", "Richard (Bluemel), who's minding the store?" They disbanded at De Zavala Road and went back to their regular card game.

And, about then, for reasons never made clear, they disbanded. One wag suggested they could use their white robes for baptism if they ever got religion, blissfully unaware that the Bluemels were Jewish. A few years later, Eddie Igo snorted in contempt that they weren't like those "other KKKs." Naively, he announced, "If one of them tries to burn a cross in my front yard, I'll shoot him."

People moved in. By the end of World War II, Stringtown was becoming only a memory for older-timers. Since it was never a visible entity as an entity—there was no civic water tower displaying the name—when it slowly faded away and died, nobody noticed. But years later a few old-timers still mentioned it. Even they are gone now.

Time's scythe changed everything. Stutts's home has been replaced by a CVS Pharmacy. The Skeleton used to stand where a Shell convenience store now sits. Fields between the low hills now have stand-alone businesses: tires, tile, etc. Four or five cattle tanks, three dairy barns, and four single-use hay barns have given way to subdivisions, Babcock North and Ox-Bow. The large field between

Stringtown and the Leon Creek, nearly a mile away, is now a grid of houses and Boone Elementary School. That cornfield supplied Piercy Benke with bushels of roasting ears (ro-sneers) that she gave to householders up and down Stringtown.

Anton Woller's house has given way to a triple storefront, offering martial arts classes. Mina Woller's house became the parking lot for the large University Baptist Church. Mrs. Hoffman's rent house and small field a greenhouse and nursery and a barracks-like renegade church with a minuscule congregation. Mina Woller's rent house was razed, leaving only the windmill without its circular cattle trough with the large goldfish.

The Michaelson-Benke two-story house was taken apart by carpenters, not razed, in order to salvage the 8 × 8, 8 × 4, and 6 × 4 timbers said to have come from a ship. The Knudsen house, the only one with a flagstone veneer, has been a neglected rubble pile for some time. The Nanez, a wooden two-story building, the living quarters above a two-car or storage area, was razed and now has several storefronts facing Babcock Road with multiple apartment buildings behind them, along with a Pizza Hut and a foreign car repair shop. Rosetta Montgomery's house was sold to Eddie Igo. Then one Sunday morning at breakfast time, the house exploded, blowing him through their bedroom window, killing him and turning Clara's bed upside down with the mattress covering her. She survived shaken but unhurt. The area became an Albertsons, which has since closed. Where the Montgomery mini-store stood half-a-century earlier, there is a Valero convenience store.

The Braendle house has been replaced by a Walgreens, a What-A-Burger, and a set of storefronts, including Mexican lunch-only and Chinese restaurants, and a nail salon.

Two streets have been cut in from the east. The first, Melissa Ann according to talk at the time, was put in to accommodate the Sam Granato family, whose house sat way back and who named the street for their daughter. The second, Tanglewood Drive, enters another subdivision, where the Benke children used to walk to Lock Hill School.

The only Stringtown remnant still standing is Mina Woller's rent property windmill, which still turns but no longer pumps water.

It is highly likely that none of the current inhabitants has ever heard of Stringtown.

In *Hamlet* (Act I, Scene 5) Shakespeare has the Ghost say: "O . . . what a falling off was there!"

****

QED

****

INDEX